PRAISE FOR *SUCCESS AFTER SERVICE*

"Lida Citroën has done it again! *Success After Service* is a must-read for anyone transitioning from a military to a civilian career. Packed with expert advice, unbeatable tools, and exercises that will develop your 'career search' muscles and enable you to flex those muscles in your new role. Lida provides everything you'll need to create and execute your personal plan for success."
Morag Barrett, author, speaker, CEO of SkyeTeam

"Lida Citroën has provided an essential guidebook for those making the transition from the military. She has compiled an invaluable resource that poses all the right questions, provides valuable exercises, offers very practical advice, and includes insights from those who successfully navigated their own transition. *Success After Service* should be the go-to guide for those taking off their military uniform and looking for their next mission post-service. I have long believed that given the incomparable training and experience of those who have served our country, if we share with them the rules of the post-service game, they will undoubtedly outplay the rest of us every time. Lida just gave them the rule book."
Maureen Casey, Chief Operating Officer, Institute for Veterans and Military Families at Syracuse University

"Ask any veteran and they'll tell you they wish they'd had a single transition resource which pulled together a clear and empowering step-by-step roadmap to a rewarding post-military life. Now there is! *Success After Service* is packed with cases studies, examples, and stories from various veteran experiences, and offers practical, inspiring, and realistic systems and tools the reader can use to build and grow a successful career after the military. As a veteran myself, I wish I had this resource available to me during my transition. It would have made my life a lot easier!"
Mike Figliuolo, Managing Director, thoughtLEADERS, LLC, and author of *One Piece of Paper*, *Lead Inside the Box*, and *The Elegant Pitch*

"Transitioning from the military into the civilian world is often challenging for our service members, but in times of economic uncertainty, the transition is considerably more difficult and requires a greater number of resources. Lida Citroën's book is more important today than ever before."
Sidney E. Goodfriend, Founder and Chairman, American Corporate Partners

"Lida Citroën has quickly become the go-to authority for personal branding and career transition. Her book is a must-read for anyone transitioning from military to civilian life. She is incredibly skilled at taking a normally complex time of life and breaking it down into chunks that are navigable and easy to win."
Myron Pincomb, CEO and Board Chairman, International Board of Credentialing and Continuing Education Standards

"Every transitioning service member should add these strategies to their toolkit. After getting off active duty, it took me eight years and four jobs before I was able to find a career path. This book would have helped me find my direction much earlier in my civilian career. Higher education is much more than earning a degree. For a veteran it is an opportunity to practice skills needed to be a successful civilian. The strategies presented by Lida provide a practical pathway to examine and guide your personal transition. The change from military service to veteran can be difficult. Lida provides a practical pathway to examine and guide your transition in order to help you eliminate or more easily overcome challenges."
Jamie Richards, Director, Veterans Success Center, Purdue University

"Lida Citroën has captured the civilian model of task and purpose in a quintessential toolkit that will resonate with all ranks as they navigate the rough seas of transition."
James Rodriguez, Former Deputy Assistant Secretary of Defense, The Office of Warrior Care Policy

Success After Service

How to Take Control of Your Job Search and Career After Military Duty

Lida Citroën

KoganPage

First published in Great Britain and the United States in 2021 by Kogan Page Limited

2nd Floor, 45 Gee Street	122 W 27th St, 10th Floor	4737/23 Ansari Road
London	New York, NY 10001	Daryaganj
EC1V 3RS	USA	New Delhi 110002
United Kingdom		India

www.koganpage.com

Kogan Page books are printed on paper from sustainable forests.

ISBNs

Hardback   978 1 78966 595 6
Paperback   978 1 78966 593 2
Ebook   978 1 78966 594 9

Library of Congress Cataloging-in-Publication Data

Names: Citroën, Lida, author.
Title: Success after service: how to take control of your job search and
    career after military duty / Lida Citroën.
Description: London; New York, NY: Kogan Page, 2020. | Includes
    bibliographical references and index.
Identifiers: LCCN 2020031583 (print) | LCCN 2020031584 (ebook) | ISBN
    9781789665956 (hardback) | ISBN 9781789665932 (paperback) | ISBN
    9781789665949 (ebook)
Subjects: LCSH: Veterans–Employment–United States–Handbooks, manuals,
    etc. | Veterans–Vocational guidance–United States. | Career
    changes–United States–Handbooks, manuals, etc. | Job hunting–United
    States–Handbooks, manuals, etc.
Classification: LCC UB357 .C55 2020 (print) | LCC UB357 (ebook) | DDC
    650.1086/970973–dc23
LC record available at https://lccn.loc.gov/2020031583
LC ebook record available at https://lccn.loc.gov/2020031584

British Library Cataloguing-in-Publication Data

A CIP record for this book is available from the British Library.

Typeset by Integra Software Services, Pondicherry
Print production managed by Jellyfish
Printed and bound by CPI Group (UK) Ltd, Croydon CR0 4YY

For Dad

CONTENTS

ABOUT THE AUTHOR

After a 20-year career in corporate America, where she helped build the brands of global companies, service firms, and nonprofit organizations, Lida Citroën launched her firm, LIDA360, LLC, in 2008. She set out to leverage her expertise as a reputation management and brand specialist to help international executives, professionals, and entrepreneurs position themselves more thoughtfully, pivot their reputation to new careers, and repair their image and reputation in complex marketplaces. As a professional speaker, executive consultant, and author, Citroën empowers others to build and manage impactful reputations to drive meaningful influence, inspiration, and impact.

In 2009, Citroën learned of the struggles of military veterans reintegrating into civilian careers, and she committed to help. As she grew her corporate business, Citroën volunteered with national programs, events, initiatives, and organizations where she taught workshops in personal branding, online positioning, and reputation management to transitioning service members and veterans.

Citroën began speaking and coaching onsite at military installations and events across the country. In 2014, she started teaching a monthly course on personal branding and LinkedIn at the United States Air Force Academy and began freelance writing on career transition for Military.com (powered by Monster.com).

In 2015, Citroën published her second book—this one for the military community—*Your Next Mission: A Personal Branding Guide for the Military-to-Civilian Transition*, which also gained attention from the human resource community that struggled to hire, onboard, and retain former military. A civilian with a business background, Citroën's ability to understand, relate to, and advocate for veterans soon had her consulting with, and presenting to, corporations and conferences of human resources professionals. Citroën presented her program, "Creating the Business Case for Hiring Veterans," at national hiring conferences to audiences of human resource professionals. She also speaks regularly at the Student Veterans of America annual conference and annual leadership events.

In collaboration with LinkedIn Learning, Citroën created numerous instructional courses sharing aspects of personal branding and reputation management. Two of her courses are focused on veterans in transition and the employers who seek to hire them.

Citroën's 2016 TEDx Talk, *The Power of Gratitude and Generosity— Serving Those Who Serve*, continues to be popular with the military community who appreciate her passion for transition resources and highlighting of important issues facing veterans leaving the military. In 2017, Citroën published her third book, *Engaging with Veteran Talent: A Quick and Practical Guide to Sourcing, Hiring, Onboarding, and Developing Veteran Employees*, a resource guide for human resources professionals seeking to hire military veteran job applicants.

Citroën has been featured for her work in media including the *Guardian* (UK), the *New York Post*, *Handelsblatt*, MSNBC, CBN Television, *U.S. News & World Report*, NBC News, *Entrepreneur*, *Military Times*, *CEO Magazine*, and numerous other media, podcasts, and websites.

A graduate of Pomona College in Claremont, California, Citroën is the recipient of several awards for her work and community leadership, including the prestigious Beatrice Montoya Award for her service to the veteran community. She continues to regularly mentor veterans, military spouses, and service members through Veterati.com.

ACKNOWLEDGMENTS

A book like this is possible only with the help, input, stories, and patience of numerous friends and colleagues who believe in this mission. I'm particularly grateful to these individuals for their assistance in ensuring we help service members and veterans find success after service:

Kevin Preston (USA, Ret.), Duane France (USA, Ret.), Lauren Addy, Adae Fonseca (USANG, Ret.), Jan Rutherford (USA), Chris Sanchez (USN, Ret.), Doug Bartels (USAF), Justin Constantine (USMC, Ret.), Justin Nassiri (USN), Byron Chen (USMC), Dave Bradt (USMC, Ret.), Patty "Tricia" Kim, Donna Chavez, Lisa Rosser (USA, Ret.), Beau Saltz, Frank Handoe (USA, Ret.), David Resilien (USMC, Ret.), Matthew Kuta (USAF, Ret.), Randall Niznick (USN, Ret.), Bryan Dyer (USN), Cesare Wright, Max Dubroff (USAF, Ret.), Chris McGraw (USA), Kristina Guerrero (USAF), Sean Brown (USMC), Susan Scotts, William Lu (USN), Heather Ehle, Daniel Rau (USMC), Diana Tsai Rau, Calvin Jensen (USMC), and Robert Barea (USA, Ret.).

And thank you to my loving family who've supported me on every step of my journey and commitment to serve those who've served.

Introduction

"I wish I'd started my transition sooner."
"Civilians don't know what we've been through."
"I didn't know what I didn't know."
"How do I figure out what comes next?"

The transition from a military to civilian career is a deeply personal and individual process filled with emotions, strategies, tactics, and beliefs. Add to this the family and peer and societal pressures, and you have created the perfect storm for stress.

My colleague Duane France (USA, Ret.) is a licensed clinical mental health counselor focused on veteran issues. He talks about the psychology of transition and how veterans approaching separation are met with unfamiliar feelings of excitement and anxiety. "They'll recognize that while the military does an exceptional job training and transitioning them for the jobs and culture of the military, they might feel unprepared for what comes next, after your military career," he shares. This is completely normal.

According to France, veterans struggle with the civilian transition in three core areas. First, they long to remain part of the collective culture of the military. Transitioning to a civilian life can feel like culture shock, but this shock can be anticipated, managed, and accepted with proper tools and knowledge. Second, the difference in values between military and civilian culture can be disruptive to a veteran's belief system. In the military, service members operate in a mission-focused collective mindset that says "Just get the job done." Now veterans might find themselves in more process-driven business environments where the values and problem-solving approach look vastly different. Last, veterans miss the shared experience they have with others in the military when they enter civilian life. People build relationships by sharing common experiences and knowledge. When a veteran works alongside a nonveteran, their different pasts, experiences, and understandings can be a barrier to building relationships.

The struggles veterans face during their transition often show up in common social miscues and missteps when interacting with nonveterans. France reminds us that the veteran uses profanity in their speech and is comfortable with dark humor. The civilian then asks inappropriate questions, such as "Have you ever killed anyone?" And the struggle to relate intensifies.

As a veteran, you can navigate the psychology of the transition by accepting that there will be challenges and issues, by committing to resolving those issues and addressing the problems, and then by working on changing the behaviors and beliefs needed to thrive in the civilian sector.

In writing this book, my goal is to provide you with the tools, ideas, insights, and resources to help alleviate the stress, reveal the possibilities, and empower you to see the opportunities in your post-military career.

Why I Wrote This Book

It's been said, "Before someone can care about what you do, they must understand why YOU care about what you do." I care about you, the military community, for many reasons.

My parents immigrated to this country before I was born. After the wars in Europe ended, my parents were finally able to leave their homeland. My father came from Holland and my mother arrived in the United States from Hungary. For as long as I remember, my mother would tell my brother and me about life in a communist state (as Hungary had become) and remind us, "Freedom isn't free." Those stories instilled a desire in me to show gratitude for my freedom in whatever way I could.

In 2009, I learned that unlike the courses available for my civilian colleagues and peers and the corporate clients I teach and coach, no one was teaching military service members and veterans about the power of personal branding and self-marketing. I raised my hand (figuratively) and decided I would help. It was not easy to make inroads into the military as a civilian. The military community is protective of its own, and I was a civilian with no personal connection. I understood the suspicion.

I started teaching and training service members and veterans and saw the impact that the training and resources I provided made in their transition and reintegration. I knew that this was my way to thank you and your families for raising your hand to serve our country and protect my freedom.

Over the following years, I began teaching and training active-duty service members and veterans across the United States at conferences, events, and corporate functions and on military installations. In 2014, I started volunteering to teach my personal branding and transition courses monthly in the TAP program at the United States Air Force Academy in Colorado Springs. In 2014, I also published my book, *Your Next Mission: A Personal Branding Guide for the Military-to-Civilian Transition*, offering tools for military personnel to identify and build their individual brands. This book garnered the attention of the media, who found it interesting that a civilian—me—could create a tool so important for veterans—you. The book also attracted many business leaders to my work, and soon I was training corporate hiring managers and recruiters on the nuances, challenges, and opportunities of the veteran employee. In 2017, I published my book, *Engaging with Veteran Talent: A Quick and Practical Guide to Sourcing, Hiring, Onboarding, and Developing Veteran Employees*, to the delight of hiring managers and recruiters who needed an accessible resource. I was consulting and speaking to large groups of human resource professionals, teaching them how to make a business case for, and steps to, hire and retain military veterans.

I became a freelance contributor at Military.com, where I write career transition articles, and I have become recognized for my practical and unique insights into reintegration. In 2015, I began working with the team at LinkedIn to develop content that met the needs of transitioning veterans and the companies seeking to hire them. Two of my courses on LinkedIn Learning focus on supporting the military community.

Success After Service is not about my journey as I've never served in uniform. This book is the collective insight of thousands of military service members, veterans, spouses, and advocates I've worked with over the years, who've shared their fears, hopes, challenges, and successes with me so I'd share it with others. The purpose of this book is to ensure your smooth and confident transition to a meaningful, productive, and happy life after the military.

My hope for this book is that it helps you make a career transition in which you understand your options, get clear on what you want, make choices that are aligned with what you value, and create a career plan so you can begin moving forward.

How to Read This Book

As you navigate *Success After Service*, personalize the information to your needs, goals, family, and career. Each recommendation, tip, and insight is designed to offer you guidance, but the implementation needs to be customized to your situation and goals. You are now in charge of your career and can make intentional and thoughtful choices with confidence given the information contained here.

This book will uncover many of the norms of civilian versus military culture, showcase opportunities, tools, and resources to grab as they present themselves to you, and help you identify blind spots and obstacles that could slow you down or divert your attention. I'll show you how to evaluate the choice of pursuing employment, education, or entrepreneurship after the military. We'll walk through how to gather and create career assets, such as a resume, cover letter, network of contacts, online presence, and post-military wardrobe.

The examples and stories presented here are shared with you by individuals who wanted you to hear their story and learn from it. Sometimes they want you to learn from their mistakes; in other cases they want you to see opportunities and evaluate choices differently. Each person who contributed to this book shared from their heart, often reliving painful aspects and lessons of their own transition.

As you work through the exercises and information contained in *Success After Service*, resist the temptation to confirm your own biases. You will naturally seek proof of your beliefs, thoughts, or suppositions as you read, and this can cause you to miss important ideas or resources. Instead, keep an open mind, consider the information presented and the suggestions offered, and make your own decision on how to progress forward. This is where you get control over your career and life!

This book is a tool to give you control and information. With information comes power. You have insight into best practices, rules, systems, and ideas that are not always talked about. Use them to your advantage to ensure your post-military career provides you with the purpose and meaning you deserve.

Thank you for your service.

Fundamentals of Career Readiness

You now have a new mission. In the same way you're given new orders in the military—a new change of command, new squad/unit/platoon/company, new location—you have a new mission, and this one is very different. Now it's about you, your family, your career, your future, your happiness, your goals. This may be the first time in your career, or life, when you've been asked to consider yourself and your desires and needs. And it may feel overwhelming. That's completely normal.

This chapter—and those that follow—will prepare you for the next step in your career mentally, emotionally, and physically. To start, I outline the goals of the military's Transition Assistance Program (TAP) and "career readiness" for this next stage and how you can mentally prepare yourself by understanding what you can, and can't, control. Next, we'll look at how to evaluate the career landscape and walk through your civilian career options, including entrepreneurship, education, and employment, after leaving the military. Finally, I'll provide guidance on how to pull it all together into a primary and secondary career path and then execute your strategy toward that path.

TAP and Career Readiness

It's my hope that you began to think about your post-military career on the first day of boot camp or officer training school—long before you hand in your separation papers. The military did not promise you a lifelong career, and you knew the day would come when you would leave. Even if you didn't think about your post-military career until many years later, getting ready to transition should start much earlier than when you pack that first box for your last duty station.

The United States Department of Defense defines career readiness and the accompanying Career Readiness Standards as the measurable outcomes which indicate your preparedness for a civilian career—regardless of your occupational field or military branch. The Department of Defense created and refined the program TAP to include core curriculum and additional modules on education, career exploration and planning, and entrepreneurship. Beginning with individual counseling and ending with a capstone event, TAP is designed to assist your transition. There are additional layers of training for service members pursuing higher education or technical training after leaving the military.

TAP gives you exposure to, and understanding of, many aspects of the transition you'll need to be career ready, whether you chose private sector employment, entrepreneurship, or education. Through the pre-separation stages of TAP, the classroom work, and the online tools, you hear from Department of Labor specialists and industry experts about navigating the available resources and insights to help you identify career paths, demilitarize your military experiences (translating military occupational codes into civilian job titles), create a resume, learn interview tips, and receive guidance for building online profiles. You may also hear from corporate professionals, government workers, and nonprofit employees who can help you see the "real world" from their perspective. These individuals may provide instruction and resources around networking, social media, accessing mentoring, and coaching and other skills. Finally, TAP empowers you with tools and processes for accessing your military benefits, including healthcare, pay, GI Bill funds, and more.

A successful career transition means you see the future clearly (or at least as clearly as you can with the information available to you), have a plan for moving through various stages of your next job, and possess the tools and resources you'll need to leverage along the way. While having a resume, network of contacts, and online profiles is important, gaining clarity in your career direction and building intention and focus on how to achieve your goals is also a big part in what comes next.

Understanding What You Can (and Can't) Control

In uniform, there was an expectedness, a predictability, to the processes and systems in which you operated. Now there are none. There are no rules, guides, or standards. There is no manual to show you how to have a meaningful civilian career. At the beginning of their transition, many veterans express feeling a lack of control over their future, and this is unsettling.

The freedom you experience in the civilian world may feel overwhelming after having spent years in the military. While the military had strict guidelines, the civilian world has no singular published code of conduct to guide behavior or issue punishments or rewards.

There are aspects of your civilian career you can control, and others you can't. For instance, you can't control other people's behavior. Every individual has their own way of acting, making decisions, and evaluating options. And companies are similarly unique—when you get a job in a company, you are dealing with unpredictable and emotion-laden individuals, not a company ("building") making decisions on your behalf.

You can control yourself. You can influence, inspire, and impact how others perceive, evaluate, and judge you, and that has a direct impact on your career success. For instance, if recruiters perceive you to be unapproachable and stubborn, they may not want to advance you in the hiring process. If networking contacts see you as someone worth taking a chance on, they will advocate for you to their network.

You can control your personal brand. Your personal brand is revealed by how you present yourself, your narrative, relationships, posture, wardrobe, elevator pitch, LinkedIn profile, and resume. Promoting a solid and memorable personal brand, through a compelling and consistent attitude, ensures that others can trust you, will endorse and refer you, and will want to work with you going forward. I'll show you how to build and drive your brand in Chapter 4.

You Can Control Your Attitude

As you transition out of the military, you'll inventory your assets, gather your tools, and tap into available resources. But one thing really matters and makes the difference between a successful next career and a struggle: your attitude.

Studies show that beliefs drive behavior, and attitude and mindset shape beliefs. Limiting beliefs ("This will be hard" or "I'm not prepared") will mean you see your transition as fraught with obstacles and frustration, and you'll struggle and likely come across as angry. If you view your future as a learning adventure full of opportunity and new prospects, you'll likely communicate optimism and approachability.

A colleague of mine who leads veteran hiring for a large company describes it this way: "I can always spot the 'angry veteran.' They're the one with a chip on their shoulder, frustrated and confused about what they want, what they can offer, and how to promote themselves. Instead of being open-minded and receptive, they come across as defensive and unpleasant. That's not the person we want to hire."

Keeping a positive outlook will be hard as you navigate the next steps. You'll find yourself doubting your decisions and questioning what to do. That's part of the process. Try to reframe your narrative ("This is all part of the transition...") and avoid doom and gloom ("I'll never get a job"). Doing so will give you a much better chance of attracting a great career opportunity, building networking relationships with people who'll want to support, endorse, and advocate for you, and feeling more intentional about your career choices.

Justin Nassiri (USN) hosts the podcast *Beyond the Uniform*, focused on success after military duty. Across the many interviews he's conducted, he sees consistent aspects of transition veterans struggle with. "You are moving from a culture, community, and work style that is familiar, understandable, and for which you have been well trained," Nassiri offers. "You know what you need to know to successfully complete your work (and mission), and you know how to access resources, tools, and problem-solving skills you'd need to work through the unexpected.

"Now you are looking at a culture, community, and work style that may feel wholly unfamiliar. It is normal for this to feel unsettling and confusing," says Nassiri. "To navigate a successful career transition, you will need to rely on your attitude and outlook as much as your skills and experience. Much of your success will be driven by your grit, persistence, and resilience… as well as your ability to clearly and confidently communicate who you are and what you can offer to a target audience."

You Can Make Choices

Having choices and options is highly desirable to civilians. From early in our careers (or maybe even during school), civilians are encouraged to stay ahead of evolving trends to remain relevant and attract choice whenever possible ("Keep your options open"). Choice, to a civilian, is power: It's the authority to choose which job to take, which promotion to pursue and accept, which team to align with, and which career goals to pursue.

Coming from the military culture, choice might not be as familiar to you and may, in fact, be a bit frightening. Many of the veterans I've coached over the years tell me that choice can feel paralyzing. They've shared that they don't feel informed or empowered to be able to take advantage of choices, let alone drive them.

I see this firsthand in my work with veterans. Since 2014, each month I volunteer to teach my program, Personal Branding for the Military-to-Civilian Transition, in the TAP program at the US Air Force Academy. I teach on the first day of the TAP program, and just before I present, the group has completed an exercise: They are asked to share what they are most excited about in transitioning to the civilian sector and then what they are most anxious about. Each month, I look at a sheet hanging up in the classroom, and one word/thought/concept is consistently listed: choice.

The group lists things they are excited about, including:

- I can determine what time I get up in the morning!
- I can decide where I want to work!
- I can choose how I dress!

Then comes the other side of the list: What are you most anxious about in leaving the military?

- I don't know what time to get up.
- I don't know what I want to do next.
- I don't know how to dress.

While these choices might not sound challenging to a civilian, they are to a veteran. These are normal concerns, and getting through the myriad of choices you'll be faced with is a part of the transition—every other veteran in your situation has experienced the same feelings. I am confident that, with the right tools and training, you will see choice and the choices of your transition with more confidence and clarity.

You Can Define a New Mission for Yourself

Transition, by nature, is filled with anticipation, fear, excitement, and curiosity. Whether you are transitioning from a career as a surgeon to one as an author, from a manager into leadership, or from the military to the private sector, often there is more that is new and different than that is familiar and the same as what you did before.

I recall how an Army combat medic, now an emergency room (ER) trauma doctor, described the transition:

On the battlefield, you quickly assess a soldier's injuries, determine the best triage, anticipate a positive outcome, and treat the patient as you are trained, medically. This is similar to how I now receive, evaluate, and prescribe treatment in the ER when someone comes through the doors. The biggest difference, however, is that in combat, we share a common patriotic mission. We are united around the "cause" and why we are in the environment, navigating the same threat, rallying for the same outcome. In my work as a hospital doctor, my patients aren't coming to me with that same patriotic grounding we shared in uniform. The tasks are very similar (treat the patient), but the mission is different (it's my job as a doctor to treat my patient).

What this doctor describes is a common thread of military-to-civilian transition: Even when the work is the similar (i.e., pilot in the Air Force and pilot for a commercial airliner, or logistician in the Air Force and fleet manager for a school district), the mission feels very different. It is not uncommon for veterans to feel conflicted around that difference, sharing:

- My civilian counterparts appear to be mostly concerned with advancing their own careers.
- My employer cares more about making money than helping our customers.
- My community says it wants to support veterans, but the resources are sparse and inadequate.

Be careful about the narrative you tell yourself about your mission going forward. You are coming from a culture and work style that is highly focused on process, procedure, and values: all ingredients needed to complete a successful mission. However, resist imposing your own sense of mission on others. Focus on yourself and what you can offer.

You Can Define Your Goals and Personal Success

Goals are critical to being able to navigate what you're working toward. Without a goal, how will you know if you're on the right path or have achieved success?

Goals can be short term (I want to meet five new professional contacts this month) or long term (I want to own a company one day). Goals can be detailed, with incremental benchmarks and milestones to achieve along the way (first I will do this, then I'll do this, then I'll move to this...), or they can be more aspirational in nature

(I want to make the people around me feel inspired.) A good combination of short-term and long-term goals, which are both tactical and aspirational, is healthy.

Similarly, your post-military career readiness requires you to consider and define your own version of what success will look like for you: What do *you* want? For many of you, this simple question is daunting. In uniform, you weren't counseled to reflect on your personal goals, or to dream about your future, or even to contemplate your purpose for being here on Earth. You were trained to do a task or skill or complete a mission, and that training ensured the protection of your troops and, ultimately, the United States.

Now I'm asking you to think about you and your future. I'll ask you this again—repeatedly through this book—because the question is not familiar to you today, but it needs to be. You need to be crystal clear on what you want to be able to pursue in the civilian sector.

For now, consider how you'll define success in five areas:

1 Personal. What will make you happy? Would spending more time with family bring you joy? What if you could have time to pursue a hobby or interest—would that make you happy? Is being able to continue to work alongside veterans important to you? Consider your personal goals to be things that are personally meaningful to you, regardless of whether they make money, have status, or are a continuation of what you've done before.

2 Professional. Is it important to you that your next job offer you an impressive job title or the ability to influence large groups of people? Are you looking to retire in 5, 10, or 15 years—what will that look like for you? Clarify your professional goals as best you can, identifying not only the type of work you will do but also the impact of that work on yourself and others.

3 Financial. This goal may require a conversation with your family. Given your military benefits and personal savings, what financial income will you need to generate to maintain or elevate your family's standard of living and prepare for your future? Consider housing, children's needs, your spouse's career aspirations, travel, and hobbies you'll want to afford. It is acceptable to have short-term and long-term financial goals, particularly if your next career move is highly uncertain.

4 Health. What is important for your health going forward? If access to ongoing medical care is warranted, this could influence where you relocate and work. If being able to live a healthy life-style with outdoor exercise on a regular basis is important to you, then you may choose to work and reside in an area that supports this. How will you determine success in meeting the needs of your health?

5 Spiritual. What goals do you have around your spiritual health? If you joined the military because of a call to serve, and that call is part of your spiritual commitment, how will you maintain that post-military? Will you join a congregation or community where others feel the same? Can you stay connected to veterans to maintain the spiritual camaraderie you felt in the military? Keep this goal as part of your overall strategy to define success to ensure you stay healthy.

As you work through this book, write down your notes and create a picture of what success will look like for you. Does a post-military career mean better work/life balance (more time with family and pursuing your hobbies)? Do you see success as financial independence? Does success mean working for a company with a famous or familiar name? Does it mean a regular paycheck?

For each goal, consider a goal sheet where you'll inventory and capture your ideas and the steps needed to achieve those goals. Here's a sample of what your goal sheet might look like to work through questions, issues, and ideas presented here.

While articulating your goals does not guarantee you will achieve them, without goals it is challenging to navigate the decision-making process and evaluate various options. If every option presented to you carries equal weight and possibility, you can be stunted in creating a path forward that is right for you and your career.

Figure 1.1 Sample Goal Sheet

Goal:_____

Start date: _____ Desired completion date: _____

Why is this goal meaningful or important?_____
_____

Benefits I'll receive from achieving the goal: _____
_____

Action steps to achieve the goal:
  1. _____
  2. _____
  3. _____
  4. _____
  5. _____

Obstacles I might encounter:_____
_____

How will I navigate the obstacles?_____
_____

Who will I need help from to achieve this goal?_____
_____

How will I recognize success?_____
_____

Assessing the Career Landscape

With a clear understanding of the situations and conditions you'll likely face—and an appreciation for what you can control and what you must accept—you can start to take action to create a post-military career. The first step is evaluating your career options within the current workplace landscape.

Career options today are endless. Technology, science, the arts, and human behavior have shaped and reshaped culture and work globally. As a result, new career paths are popping up every day. The good news is that you have many promising options for a career path that aligns your skills, passion, and talents in ways previous generations could only imagine.

Today, transitioning veterans entering the civilian world can choose from entrepreneurship, higher education, work in the private sector, or working for the government, for a start. Here I'll provide a short introduction to each of these career options so that you can consider which option sounds most appealing to you and investigate it further.

Is Entrepreneurship Calling You?

Many veterans are attracted to business ownership and entrepreneurship after leaving their military career. In fact, research by the US Small Business Administration shows that military service gives veterans advantages in self-employment and that veterans are 45 percent more likely to be entrepreneurs compared to nonveterans. In 2017, 2.5 million veteran-owned businesses made up about 9 percent of business ownership in the United States.

Veterans are well suited for self-employment and business ownership in part due to many of the character traits, skills, and training received during military service. For instance, we know that veterans are resilient and tenacious—critical factors in seeing a business grow from inception to viability. Veterans have demonstrated leadership qualities, which are critical to promoting and selling the business idea to investors, business partners, and employees. Veterans bring a strong work ethic, excellent problem-solving skills, and the patience to see the mission through to completion—all important traits to enable a person to navigate the highs and lows of business ownership.

I often describe myself as an accidental entrepreneur: I never wanted to own my own company or had visions of being my own boss. I wasn't a risk taker, and never saw myself as a visionary for a mission I created. But in 2008, when I was faced with the decision to get another job or start something new on my own, I became more interested in being a business owner. I started my company in the midst of the global financial collapse, when everyone around me was either losing their jobs or desperately trying to hold onto theirs. The nature of my business was helping global professionals become more valuable to their employers or stakeholders—a message that resonated well in the times—and the business became a success.

Today I counsel entrepreneurs to evaluate this career path carefully, taking in the full breadth of what's involved and what's realistic, and weighing the pros and cons of self-employment. Yes, it's great to make your own schedule, work as hard (or little) as you want, and be accountable to no one but yourself. But being an entrepreneur is so much more than that!

Let's examine some realities of entrepreneurship. How would you respond to the following questions?

- **Are you self-motivated and work well independently?** Can you craft a vision, then set a strategy and tactics to meet that vision? If you're more comfortable being given direction and rules, understand that entrepreneurship is 100 percent accountability and responsibility for the success of the business or venture.

- **Do you have a healthy network of allies, partners, vendors, possible investors, coaches, and advocates who will hold you accountable to meet your goals and will support you along the way?** While self-employment often means working solo, you need other people to endorse, refer, invest in, and coach you along the way.

- **Are you self-disciplined?** Personally, I can attest to the temptation I struggle with when I need to prepare financial statements or inventory books and I'd rather being taking a walk in my neighborhood or scouring the internet for a sale on shoes. Having self-discipline to manage your time well and prioritize your day is very important.

- **Are you a saver or a spender?** When you run your own company, what you earn is yours after you pay expenses. You are in control of how much you earn and keep. No one takes a percentage of your revenues. If you aren't accustomed to saving and investing in the business, and yourself, it can be easy to spend money as fast as you make it, making the business vulnerable.

- **Do you consider yourself a risk taker?** Are you comfortable with uncertainty and unfamiliarity? There is plenty of that in entrepreneurship. Nothing is guaranteed, and just when you think you've figured things out, things change. If risk and uncertainty excite you (or at least don't terrify you), that's a good sign!

- **Are you a social person?** Many entrepreneurs are surprised at how lonely the work can be. Sure, your business can employ people, you can have customers, vendors, and business partners, but ultimately, it's you that runs the show and makes the decisions. For some new entrepreneurs, the lack of camaraderie leads them back to more traditional work.

Would More Education Be a Good Next Step?

Pursuing education after the military is a popular choice. The Department of Defense provides you with many benefits, including advanced education benefits. Originally called the Servicemen's Readjustment Act of 1944, the GI Bill was designed to support World War II veterans as they rebuilt their post-military lives.

In 2008, President George W. Bush signed into effect the Post-911 GI Bill, expanding and clarifying benefits awarded to veterans. As the US Department of Veterans Affairs states:

> If you have at least 90 days of aggregate active duty service after Sept. 10, 2001, and are still on active duty, or if you are an honorably discharged Veteran or were discharged with a service-connected disability after 30 days, you may be eligible for this VA-administered program. Purple Heart recipients, regardless of length of service, are qualified for Post-9/11 benefits at the 100 percent level. Certain members of the Reserves who lost education benefits when REAP was sunset in November 2015, may also be eligible to receive restored benefits under the Post-9/11 GI Bill.[1]

Benefits under the Post-911 GI Bill include 100 percent reimbursement of tuition and fees, a monthly housing allowance, and a stipend for books and school supplies.

Since 2009, veterans have earned 453,000 degrees and certificates using their GI Bill.

> The most popular degrees are in the fields of Business, Management, Marketing, Health, and Liberal Arts and Sciences. We also know that Veterans show a 72 percent success rate in higher education,

with 25 percent of student Veterans achieving multiple degrees or certifications. Estimates are that by 2029 1.4 million advanced degrees will have been awarded using GI Bill support.[2]

Veterans with bachelor's degrees on average earn more than their civilian counterparts ($84,255 versus $67,232), and veterans with advanced degrees also outpace their peers on average ($129,082 for veterans compared to $99,734 for nonmilitary).[3]

Some reasons you might consider education after military service include:

- You aren't certain about your career and want exposure to more options, career choices, professions, opportunities.

- You are entering a competitive field where a bachelor's or master's degree is needed, and you don't have one.

- You seek to launch your next career with more advanced education in your field.

- You are changing the focus of your work, and certifications in the new field will give you a better starting point.

There are many educational tracks to consider for advanced degrees: Want to own your own business? Why not look into an innovation and entrepreneurship degree? Passionate about project management? Consider getting your certification to be a Project Management Professional? If you decide your career path will include advanced education, you will find yourself in good company.

Pursuing Work in the Private Sector

The "private sector" describes businesses and organizations that are nongovernmental and are not publicly owned and operated. Most of the approximately 200,000 service members who are transitioning out of the military each year end up choosing a career in the private sector, which also encompasses nonprofit organizations and public companies.

Private sector companies rarely follow consistent norms, rules, systems, or terminology from one to the next, although there may be patterns based on industry.

For instance:

- "Technology start-up company" (early-stage companies focused on technology solutions or software) could describe two people working in their garage or it can refer to a growing company with 50 employees, several investors, and multiple rounds of funding.

- "Healthcare company" could refer to an insurance provider focused on medical coverage, a medical device company, or a consulting firm offering process improvement to hospitals.

- "Financial firm" may mean an accounting firm, investment or brokerage house, individual financial planning coach, or training program targeting at-risk kids and financial fitness.

- "Nonprofits" (or "not-for-profit entities") serve a mission. They are focused on mission over profits, but revenues still matter. It's often a misperception that you can't earn a good living working in a nonprofit. Although generating profits is not a goal of nonprofits, that doesn't mean they all operate on a shoestring.

Bottom line, within every industry, there are subsets of companies doing interesting work. To say you are attracted to finance is like saying you like dessert; it's really not specific.

For veterans entering the private sector, the opportunities are endless. From consulting, to management, to skilled labor, to executive leadership, veterans are well poised to translate many of the trainings and experiences from the military into their civilian pursuits. Savvy employers recognize that you can train on skills but not on character. The soft skills and personality traits you developed in the military typically can't be taught on the job. Employers see this as a benefit to hiring veterans.

Is Government Work Right for You?

The United States government is the largest employer in the country. Many service members pursue work in the federal system as a General Service (GS) employee, likely because the culture and process can resemble their experience in the military—the rules are mostly consistent and predictable. A former Green Beret I coached was particularly drawn to work in city government because he felt the landscape was familiar: "I could see how decisions were being made, how engagement was built with constituents, and how planning supported overall mission. To me, this felt like an extension of the critical thinking skills I developed in the Army." Data from the US Bureau of Labor Statistics shows that in 2018, more veterans (who served after September 2001) were employed in the public sector and with the federal government than their nonveteran counterparts.[4]

Jobs in the government sector vary greatly, including everything from support positions (administrative assistant), to operational (program director), to managerial (human resources manager), to creative (communications specialist) and strategic (business development director), to jobs requiring security clearance (contracts specialist). Federal jobs typically pay competitive salaries, offer good benefits, and provide longevity on your resume, if you perform well. For many transitioning service members, the stability of the federal job is highly attractive in a time of uncertainty.

Crafting Your Career Path

With an understanding of the options you have in front of you, and based on your goals and desires, it's time to craft your career path. Your path consists of many elements, including a statement of your goals, a thoughtful and intentional mindset, a focused and useful network, and research into the industries and companies you'll pursue.

You may write your career path plan down on paper, manage it in an Excel spreadsheet, or capture it in a personal journal—whatever works best for you. However you choose to capture it, your career path plan should contain the following elements:

1 Statement of your goals:
   Write down the answer to the following question: What does success mean to me?

2 List of your professional network, their contact information, and any additional relevant information

3 A personal branding statement: What is unique about you that makes you valuable to potential employers? What is the most important thing that any potential employer/investor/academic institution needs to know about you and why? What unique value can you bring to any task that you undertake?

4 List of your personal support network—who are those people who will encourage you, mentor you, coach you, and help you stay focused and consistent?

5 List of skills you anticipate leveraging, building on, and using in your next career

6 Passions you would like to pursue after the military

7 Your timeline for making impact in the areas you'll seek to influence

Your career path plan is an iterative, fluid, and evolving tool you'll use throughout your career to assess where you are, where you're going, and what steps you will (or have) take to get there. The plan will ensure you hold yourself accountable to following the steps and building the tools you'll need, provide you with a macro look at how you're progressing (self-assessment is critical), and ensure you can course-correct and pivot as necessary based on your progress toward goals.

Table 1.1 Career Path Plan Worksheet

Year	Career Goal	Skills/ Talents I'll Use	My Value Proposition (Brand)	What I'm Most Passionate About	Key Networking Contacts (Who Will Help Me?)	Key Support Contacts (Who Will Support Me?)	Timeline Impacts or Variables
1							
2							

Your career path plan can represent a worksheet, like the one shown in Table 1.1, to keep your goals and thoughts organized. You could create separate worksheets for each goal. For instance, you may have a first career path sheet for your life as a student veteran, then another one for later, after graduation.

Designing a Primary (Plan A) and a Secondary (Plan B) Career Path

It can be helpful to look at career path options in terms of primary and secondary choices. Your primary career path, or Plan A, will be the most desirable option given your experience, readiness, network, needs, and skills. Think of this path as the story of how you will reach your career goal. Each job in your post-military career moves you closer to your career goals. If you need additional education, skills, or contacts to enter your primary career path, make sure your narrative accounts for the time, effort, and resources needed to get to your desired career state. Be sure to provide yourself with checkpoints along the way to ensure progress or make course corrections.

If your primary career path requires more extensive training, certifications, or on-the-job experience before you're ready to fully pursue it, or if family or personal reasons prevent you from pursuing Plan A initially, create a secondary career path, or a Plan B. Having a Plan B also makes sense when you are changing the nature of your work (e.g., if you were a mechanic in the Navy but now want to work as an inspirational speaker).

Here's how this path might look:

- **Primary Career Path**
  Retire – Project Management – Program Management
  a. Exit the military with a bachelor's degree, PMP certification (worked on during terminal leave), and membership in national and local project management organizations.
  b. Network into desired job, leveraging contacts in person and online.

    c. Work one to three years in mid-size company to gain real-world skills and experience. Build leadership and project management skills.

    d. Ultimate goal: Program management in international aerospace company that works with the military

- **Secondary Career Path**
  Separate – Bachelor's Degree – PMP – Internship – Junior Project Manager – Program Manager

    a. Exit the military with an honorable discharge.

    b. Attend a university to complete a bachelor's degree. Work part-time on campus to augment income.

    c. In addition to a job, pursue part-time internship (after graduation) in either operations or project management with a local company. Gain firsthand experience.

    d. Pass PMP certification (take night classes).

    e. Work as a junior project manager in a mid-size company, preferably in manufacturing or software development.

    f. Transition to aerospace in an entry-level to mid-level position.

    g. Ultimate goal: Program management in an international aerospace company that works with the military

As you can see, the goal can be the same, but the path looks different. Although these steps might mean it takes longer to secure your dream job, having a planned secondary career path helps you get closer to achieving your long-term career goals.

In Closing

Making the transition from a military career to a civilian one, or to entrepreneurship or additional education, can feel daunting. Career readiness prepares you for the unknowns by putting you in charge of your own transition: You are driving the process and mindset needed to ensure you make good choices for the next step.

    Gathering your career assets will be important as we move through this journey. Later we'll talk about translating your military skills and experience into a narrative that employers will understand and then positioning you to be a relatable and attractive candidate for companies seeking someone like you.

For now, recognize that the process starts here, right now. Whether you have 18 months or eight weeks until you start a civilian career, where you are is here.

Evaluate options (employment, education, entrepreneurship) and calmly articulate your short-term and long-term goals—personal, professional, financial, health, and spiritual—as they will provide a filter through which you can sift your options. Recognize that some aspects of your transition will be out of your control, yet many others are manageable.

Finally, grow your career having Plan A and Plan B options, to gain a sense of purpose and strategy to move forward. While there will be unexpected surprises along the way, having a plan is reassuring during this time of transition and change.

Notes

1 US Department of Veterans Affairs, Post-911 GI Bill (Chapter 33), www.benefits.va.gov/gibill/post911_gibill.asp (archived at https://perma.cc/J7YD-VWP2)

2 National Veteran Success Tracker, https://nvest.studentVeterans.org/wp-content/uploads/2017/02/NVEST_Factsheets.pdf (archived at https://perma.cc/PK8R-WS2D)

3 Institute for Veterans and Military Families, "Student Veterans," https://ivmf.syracuse.edu/wp-content/uploads/2017/09/Student-Veterans_Valuable_9.8.17_NEW.pdf (archived at https://perma.cc/HN7U-YS4L)

4 Bureau of Labor Statistics, US Department of Labor, news release, Thursday, March 19, 2020, "Employment Situation of Veterans—2019," https://www.bls.gov/news.release/pdf/vet.pdf (archived at https://perma.cc/GA46-Q34M)

What to Do Before You Separate/Retire

Whether the choice was yours or was made for you by the military, due to your health or other circumstances, it's now time to prepare for the next chapter in your life: post-military.

In all the years I have taught transition and reintegration strategies, universally the service members I've met had questions and concerns, felt intimidated and apprehensive, and approached the civilian transition hesitantly. Whether they served 4 years or 34 years, the men and women I've met said this transition felt like nothing they'd experienced before.

Getting career-ready for this transition starts by understanding the realities of what you'll (likely) face, gathering the resources you'll need before exiting the military, and organizing the job assets you'll want to catalog in order to appeal to the audiences you'll target. Here we'll discuss both the strategic and tactical steps you'll need for a successful career transition.

Realities of the Transition

It's very possible that nothing in your military career has prepared you for what will come next. Everything from the language, to the wardrobe, to the mission of your next career environment may feel foreign.

As you build your career strategy for this next chapter of your life, consider how you were trained: Top-down planning leads to bottom-up refinement. This approach will help you evaluate the culture, people, language, and community you are moving into and empower you with helpful tools, resources, and steps to navigate your career going forward.

Top-Down Planning: See the Big Picture

Let's start by understanding the landscape of the people, processes, and performance expectations of your next career so you can plan properly and accordingly for your (and your family's) goals. If you understand what's facing you, you can plan and organize your career effectively.

Civilians Are the Same Yet Different

Many years ago, I heard it said that "the military recruits from the same population as civilian employers: civilians. We were all civilians before we joined the military, and now we're going back to that community."

At some point in your life, you decided your path forward: For some of you, a family tradition of service led you to join the military right after high school. For others, ROTC was the pathway to a military career. For some service members, the military provided a path to pay for education, to travel the world, to learn skills not taught in mainstream careers, or it provided a diversion from a negative path that appeared to be coming their way. For others, the events of September 11, 2001, prompted a commitment to serve. And, just as there are numerous unique and deeply personal reasons some civilians chose to join the military, there are many reasons individuals do not choose the path of military service.

There Are More Civilians than Veterans in the Workforce

Realistically, it is most likely that, in your next career, you will work and interact predominantly with nonmilitary personnel, civilians. As approximately 2 percent of the American population has served in uniform, that means 98 percent have not. Of those who have not served, many also claim not to have a family member or close friend who has served in the military.

Why does this matter? A 2011 research study from the Pew Research Center titled *The Military-Civilian Gap: War and Sacrifice in the Post-9/11 Era* (www.pewresearch.org/wp-content/uploads/sites/3/2011/10/Veterans-report.pdf) showed that 71 percent of Americans admit they don't understand the challenges post-9/11 veterans face. Therefore, you may encounter civilians who:

- **Have formed opinions about military service from what they've seen in movies and television.** Their view of what you did while in uniform might be skewed by a Hollywood portrayal of combat, military service, and reintegration after military duty.

- **Possess a negative perception about military service.** Perhaps their political views skew their outlook on the military, or maybe they've heard that veterans have certain traits they find undesirable to work alongside, thereby stereotyping you incorrectly.

- **Act with implicit biases, positive or negative.** Whether this comes from direct experience or hearsay, some civilians believe mistruths or misperceptions about what it was like to serve and what you're bringing into the civilian sector, and they may treat you incorrectly because they see your world through that lens.

- **Feel intimidated by you.** Patriotic civilians with no connection to veterans or service members may resist engaging with you out of fear of the unknown or intimidation due to respect for your service and a desire not to offend or upset you with their ignorance about your experience.

- **Speak a different language.** Unless the civilian you're speaking with works as a civilian contractor to the military or is somehow connected to military service or transition, they likely will not understand the acronyms, jargon, or lingo veterans use. Even after more than ten years of working alongside veterans, I still need clarification on terminology, Military Occupational Specialty codes, and lingo. Imagine how frustrating or intimidating it can be for someone who is not closely working with veterans on a regular basis.

- **Want to show appreciation and respect for your service.** Although some groups are pushing back on the phrase "Thank you for your service" often used by civilians to service members and veterans, the phrase is still common. For most civilians, the expression is a genuine and heartfelt show of appreciation. Whatever your feelings about being thanked for your work, appreciate the intention.

Just as you don't know about certain nuances of the civilian sector, the people you'll work alongside are just as confused about your past experiences—the challenges and the successes.

I'm making some broad-stroke generalizations here, but they are important to consider as you ready yourself to work alongside civilians. Just as no two veterans are the same, neither are civilians. After all, we are all humans first.

Civilian Career Paths

Often civilians follow a career path that looks like:

- High school to trade school to apprenticeship to employment (and maybe entrepreneurship later)
- High school to college to employment (possible entrepreneurship later)
- High school to employment (possible entrepreneurship later)
- High school to entrepreneurship (less typical, but still statistically relevant)
- College/university to graduate school (to specialize or deepen certification and training) to employment (possible entrepreneurship later)
- College/university to employment or entrepreneurship
- Graduate school to employment, entrepreneurship or academia (teaching, administration, journalism)

Internships, apprenticeships, and entry-level careers are very common, and career changes happen at any point and may happen often during a civilian's career path.

For-Profit Versus Nonprofit Civilian Career Paths

Whether during school or afterward, civilians are often drawn to either for-profit or nonprofit careers. For-profit enterprises are run and managed with the goal of generating profit. Nonprofit (or not-for-profit) entities are structured differently, are managed by a board of directors, and typically follow a "mission-focused" purpose.

Some people join nonprofits to further a cause or purpose or to advocate for a population they feel passionately connected to. For many of these people, solving a problem or serving a community is personally fulfilling.

It's an arguable stereotype, then, that individuals who pursue for-profit work are interested in different goals. For some, this means personal financial success. For others, being able to grow a company, a product, or a service into greater market share is attractive. For still others, pursuing work in the for-profit sector is more logical given their experience, educational background, geographic location, and so on. It's not fair to assume, however, that people who pursue for-profit work are not passionate about causes, missions, and initiatives that serve communities or populations in need.

Culturally, Civilian Workstyles Differ

"Teamwork" May Feel Different

In the military, teams work as well-oiled machines. Instruction, roles, responsibilities, and shared commitment to the completion of the mission are reinforced by expert and trusted camaraderie and teamwork.

When you're in uniform, you know that the man or woman to the right, left, front, or back of you will always support you (literally and figuratively). The "got your six" practice is lived daily while you're in uniform, whether you ever see combat or not. You know that those around you will protect your life as you would theirs.

Many veterans leaving the military worry about leaving that sense of protection and shared commitment behind them. Will your civilian boss have your back the way your commanding officer did? Can you count on your team to be truthful and forthcoming if it's not in their best interest?

You may certainly encounter colleagues in the civilian sector who are more concerned with self-preservation and their own career goals than you and yours. They may even try to undermine you to push themselves ahead. Yes, unfortunately this happens.

More likely, though, you will meet teammates, supervisors, and subordinates who seek to move everyone forward, not just themselves. They will be selfless, generous, patient, and supportive of you and your goals. These individuals are concerned with keeping their job and growing their career, but not at the expense of those around them.

Problem-Solving May Feel Different

I remember the first time a veteran described how he was trained to solve problems in the military. "I didn't care about pretty. I was tasked with getting my unit from Point A to Point B, and I needed to get the problems out of the way. It wasn't the prettiest result, but we got the job done."

In the military, elegance of solution is not the goal; completing the mission is. You were trained to identify challenges, evaluate options, and push forward to solve them. Whether you worked as a driver in the advance team on frontline combat missions, evaluated supply chain efficiencies, or managed public affairs, your job was to eliminate obstacles and problems so the mission could proceed.

Now, in the civilian sector, you will be asked to solve problems with more attention to the "why" and "how" rather than the "what." To a civilian employer, it matters who gets hurt in the process of solving a budget crisis. It matters if the team doesn't feel supported as you eliminate a key position from the roster. It will matter why you fired a vendor because their product was defective and why you felt it necessary to not secure a replacement vendor. Solving the problem is essential, but the way you do it and your motivation for doing it are also important.

Asking for Help Is a Sign of Strength

When you served in uniform, you might have felt that asking for help was risky because you could expose vulnerability or reveal that your knowledge was not up to par. This put you at a disadvantage with your superiors, peers, and the troops you were responsible for.

In the civilian sector, asking for help is seen as a sign of strength and confidence. To be brave enough to solicit input, guidance, and support is admired. We respect professionals and leaders who share their vulnerabilities, who clarify expectations and ask for information when they don't know how to proceed or get something done.

You might find this awkward at first—after all, you're hired for a job you're expected to know how to do. In reality, we can't possibly know everything, and civilian culture supports team effort, reinforcements, and help.

Consider this scenario: In the military, your drill sergeant didn't start off with "Here's what I expect from you." Instead, there were established uniform standards that you knew you were expected to uphold and meet.

In the civilian sector, there are rarely published uniform standards for our work. Company leaders set business strategies, which managers and contributors work toward in their jobs. You may have questions around the business strategies or the tactical plans that your managers work toward. Clarifying and asking for help setting expectations is critical—how else can you know if you're working on the right system, moving your project in the right direction?

Many of my veteran coaching clients tell me they struggle with asking for help, particularly around expectations on the job. They are excited about a new opportunity, believe they have an idea of what their supervisors expect from them, and quickly realize there are variables they didn't consider. Instead of seeking clarification or asking their boss to spell out their expectations in granular steps, these veterans feel their confidence erode, and they often leave the company. Employers want employees to ask for clarification and assistance. They encourage employees to push past job descriptions and performance requirements to clarify what is needed to be successful (to your boss and their boss). Although your employer may not articulate this well, it will be important that you get comfortable with the notion of seeking guidance and assistance to understand and perform your job. Your civilian counterparts will be more comfortable with and accustomed to this structure of work and communications.

Image Matters—A Lot

As you begin to network and interact more with civilians outside of the military context, you'll quickly see that image matters. The optics of a company or individual often drive initial first impressions and the perception that is formed of the company or person. Companies care about how they are viewed in the general marketplace by both customers and employees. Anything that could tarnish that view is considered risky.

Individuals also put effort into their appearance and image. Since for many jobs, civilians don't wear a uniform, they can use their image as a form of self-promotion, reflecting their personality, style, and values.

Gender Relations

Many years ago, when I was teaching a large workshop of transitioning service members, a question came up from an audience member: "How likely is it that I'll work alongside females after I leave the Army?" he asked. My response: "Extremely likely."

In most jobs, in most industries, men and women work alongside each other at all levels. There are some industries and companies that are considered "predominantly male," and at the highest levels of leadership we still see a disproportionate number of men, but there are great national efforts to shift this paradigm.

If you are a male, get comfortable with the fact that you'll work together with women, possibly report to a woman, and have women as clients, investors, coaches, staff, and business partners in your next job.

Civilians May Not Understand the Culture You've Worked In

Periodically remind yourself that the civilians you'll work for, or alongside, do not have experience or context for your military work and style. They aren't wrong and you aren't right; you're all just different. Their workstyle and work ethic might look odd to you, but that doesn't make it right or wrong.

The men and women you will now collaborate with, rely on, ask for help from, and lead may question your behavior and approach from time to time. They may not comprehend or appreciate where you come from and why you act differently. For instance, they won't understand why you show up early to work ("Early is on time, on time is late."), why you stay past your shift, or why you're willing to do work that is not assigned to you. Your previous experience prepared you for work in the military context; now we need to realign your workstyle with that of your next employer.

Your civilian colleagues also may display insensitive behavior without the intention to offend. I've heard from many veterans about the thoughtless and offensive questions they were asked ("Did you kill anyone?" or "Do you agree with the decision to go to war?") from civilians. Although you may feel the urge to react strongly and negatively, consider that these questions are likely coming from a place of misinformation or ignorance, not offense.

Prepare yourself in advance for how you'll respond to challenges, questions, or statements about your service. Don't initiate conflict with people who never served a day in your boots.

Business Often Values Different Things from the Military

Culture Is King

For civilian employers, company culture is as precious as their brick-and-mortar facilities, their logos and intellectual property, and their bank accounts. Culture can make or break the viability of an enterprise.

Culture is often defined as the set of principles, beliefs, and common goals that employees ascribe to and align with. When there is a strong culture, an organization can confidently and consistently promote its values to customers, employees, and other stakeholders.

For many companies, every employee within the culture is recognized equally—from a junior staff member to the chief executive officer. Healthy cultures are ones where all employees feel empowered and appreciated and are clear on why they work at the company.

When a company has a positive culture, business productivity improves, hiring is easier (the hiring team can quickly determine whether potential new employees would fit into the culture), and retention improves—employees like working for the company and they don't want to leave. You can imagine how valuable this is to companies!

I often explain to transitioning service members the importance of culture in this way: Culture clarifies and demonstrates a company's brand. It's the personification of how the company wants the market to perceive it. For instance, if a company's brand value says it believes in treating employees well, then the culture of the company must support that. Employees would speak well of their employer on social media, there would be lines of applicants wanting to work for the company, and the website would show how much fun the employees have working for the company (which cares so much about them).

Culture reflects how a company treats its employees and how the employees treat each other. Although you'll find similarities in culture across some industries, companies like to promote a "unique" culture to the marketplace. They pride themselves on working hard to culti-vate and sustain a special environment for employees, stakeholders, and customers.

Since brand is *the expectation of an experience* a customer, em-ployee, or prospect has with the brand, culture is a critical ingredient of a successful brand. Brands make us feel something—we can trust the company or product, we feel safe with that product, we feel in-centivized to advocate for that company—and feelings are critical. Studies on human behavior show that we as humans are motivated to buy and commit based on feelings, not on logic.

Consider what I said above regarding problem-solving. The way you solve problems, the way you engage specific resources and indi-viduals in the solution, and the impact your solution has on others is critical to companies because it reflects on their brand and culture.

Business Values Innovation

Being first to market is critical in most industries. Although others may value a slower-paced business model, many US companies today focus on innovation and speed as competitive advantages.

As you exit the military, remind yourself that you have a great deal of experience in cutting-edge, innovative environments. You have tested new processes, procedures, tools, and technologies, often under stressful situations and with limited resources. Your ability to think critically under duress, pivot when needed, and reinvent established systems is extremely valuable in the civilian sector.

There is some misperception that military innovation does not have practical application in the civilian sector. This belief has been proven inaccurate, but you might run into it. Even though you may not need to create a unique satellite system to reveal covert opera-tions in hostile territories going forward, you can still draw on your training in problem-solving and innovating to help civilian compa-nies better troubleshoot their challenges.

Competition Is Seen as Healthy

Just as in sports, competition between companies is seen as a healthy expression of excellence and strategy. In business, however, the "score" isn't always obvious or revealed. In sports, viewers can follow along as plays are reflected on the scoreboard. In business, companies can inflate their success, stature, and growth, creating a misleading impression of their competitiveness.

You'll be evaluating potential employers not only for their culture, business, operations, and leadership mindset but also for their competitive positioning. If you choose to work for an industry leader, there will be perks and opportunities that come with that move. Sometimes these opportunities are seen as resume builders because of the positive way they reflect on your career path. The downside of working for a market leader could be a lack of career advancement if the company isn't risk tolerant (for fear of losing position).

You might also choose to work for a company that is lagging or struggling. This could afford you the opportunity to grow your impact in more meaningful ways, based on your role. You also run the risk of unemployment if the company isn't able to turn the struggle into viability.

As you prepare to exit the military, evaluate your readiness for your next career.

Strategic Questions to Consider

1 **How much longer will you work?** Depending on how you'll exit the military, what should your next career look like? If you're retiring and will be getting retirement pay, do you still need to make six figures? Or is that something you believe you deserve? If you're leaving the military after 20+ years, exiting as an E7 or as a senior enlisted person, do you plan to have another career? Will you need income, or are you more concerned with staying busy and looking at volunteer work? If you exit after five years, you likely want to pursue a post-military career that will grow over time and provide for retirement in 20 to 25 years.

2 **Is joining the Guard and Reserves an option?** Following your military service career, you may feel ready to leave everything about the military behind. Or you may like the Army but are tired

of relocating your family, or you seek to grow your career in different ways. Or perhaps you've had enough of the military but wish to maintain your benefits and work toward a military retirement scenario.

Joining the Guard and Reserves could be a viable option for you and your family. You'll be able to extend your benefits to include Guard and Reserve benefits to retirement at 20 years, you can supplement the health insurance benefits offered by your civilian employer, and you maintain your commitment to service of your country.

Before exiting the military, decide whether the type of civilian work you'll pursue aligns well with Guard and Reserve work. Some careers, such as police, fire fighting, and airline piloting, have schedules that work well with Guard and Reservist time commitments and schedules. Other careers, such as some corporate positions, might require more finesse and up-front conversation to ensure your work schedule will be flexible enough.

3 **Are there specific needs from your family?** Your spouse and family may have needs and goals that need to be considered. Perhaps your spouse wants to move home, closer to their family. Perhaps your child needs access to certain healthcare or educational resources. These needs must be considered as you plan your career moves forward.

4 **Do you want to do the same work?** If you served as an Army ordnance bomb disposal school commandant and want to continue this kind of work after you leave service, you might find your career options limited. If you served as a surgeon in the Air Force and want to continue practicing medicine as a surgeon, your options are more plentiful. Consider whether you want to continue your training, expertise, and work after you leave, and if your work is in high or low demand.

5 **Are you able to explain your military career?** Consider how you might communicate your transportable skills (the ones you can take with you from the military, such as problem-solving, leadership, loyalty, and resiliency) as well as those nontransportable, or military-specific, skills, such as advanced aircraft maintenance and satellite technology, if you'll change careers after separation.

6 **Are you looking at a complete career change?** If so, which certifications, trainings, and experiences will you need to complete before you enter this new career? If you are leaving the Army as a combat medic, for instance, and want to work as a business consultant, would getting your master of business administration degree speed up your entry into the business community? Are you looking at a career that requires specific certification to have influence? For example, human resources (HR) professionals can practice in HR for their entire career, but to move up the corporate ladder in many organizations, gain additional skills and insights, and build a leadership brand for themselves, they will pursue the Certified Professional or Senior Certified Professional certification from the Society of Human Resource Management, a leading national HR organization. This title reflects their training, skill, and talent as a senior professional.

You aren't simply changing jobs or even changing careers when you transition out of the military. You are moving from one culture, workplace, language, and team to another. Before you separate or retire, consider how you'll approach the transition from the highest level—from your goals, dreams, family's needs, and personal objectives. Then look at the tactical steps to complete before you take off your uniform for the last time.

Bottom-Up Planning

With a firm understanding of the strategic (big-picture) differences you'll face, you can begin to focus on the tactical steps necessary to ensure you cover all the necessary bases.

Get the Most from TAP

The Department of Defense (DoD) crafted the TAP program to meet several objectives in preparing you to separate from the military. Aside from the tools and resources you'll be provided with, there are numerous ways to take advantage of your TAP experience to grow your career.

Take advantage of these opportunities.

- **Attend every program you can.** Although certain programs are required to complete your transition requirements, others offered at your base may seem obscure. When my personal branding course was first promoted at the Air Force Academy, we were met with lukewarm reception. The program I taught during the weeklong program TAP class was to a captive audience, but we decided to add a quarterly half-day workshop to build on what I'd taught in TAP. Over time, and as word got out about the value of personal branding, my classes filled up. Transitioning airmen and service members from other bases learned about the classes and began coming over to the Academy for this training. Today there's a wait list for each workshop I teach.

  Resist the urge to judge what might feel like an ambiguous program. Your base readiness center works closely with the local community to offer programming and guest lectures from experts who volunteer their time. Learning is never a bad thing, so broaden your thinking and learn as much as you can.

- **Network.** Everyone sitting in those TAP classes with you will find a place in the civilian sector. Whether they return to school, start a business, find employment, or retire, they know other people and will continue to grow their own networks outside of the military. View this as an opportunity to jump-start your own network by learning about your peers in the class, finding areas of mutual interest or goals, and connecting with them online. Then stay in touch after you've separated. Today's classmate could become tomorrow's chief executive.

  Also, connect with your instructors online. These individuals are often well connected in broader communities and industries and can provide valuable insight and connections to others outside of the military.

- **Learn about online positioning.** You'll be exposed to the power of online tools, from the O*Net OnLine portal for career exploration tools, to LinkedIn for building your digital reputation. If you've been hesitant to join the social media community, now's the time to reconsider. Take every opportunity to learn from instructors and your peers about how to use online resources and tools to best promote yourself, research career options and companies, and grow your network outside of the military.

- **Follow up on all offers.** Several of the volunteer instructors I know who speak in various TAP programs offer additional coaching, guidance, and connection to the audience. Follow up and see what additional programs might benefit you outside of what's offered in TAP.

- **Get introduced to business writing.** Pay attention to the various ways civilians and professionals communicate. For example, note how emails are brief and succinct, voicemails are factual and repeat key information such as phone numbers, and written copy is interesting, engaging, and brief. Brevity and accuracy are important. Every communication—email, letter, text message—does not need to contain every bit of information to convey the message.

Build Your Post-Military Wardrobe

Knowing what to wear when there isn't a uniform is tricky for both men and women. I recall a conversation with a retiring Army veteran who shared her struggles in finding her image out of uniform. She described how she went to a national chain of women's career clothing and asked the young salesclerk to help her get together outfits she could wear to job interviews.

She left the store with several bags of attractive skirts, blazers, slacks, and blouses... all in either black, gray or, white. She'd heard somewhere that neutrals would give her the most options and flexibility in her career wardrobe, so she stuck with that.

She quickly learned, however, that she'd replaced one uniform (that of the Army) with another. She lacked the confidence to coordinate accessories, to add color and "flare" to her look, so she defaulted to an uninspiring wardrobe.

In another example, I recall a veteran I worked with through a transition program ask me, "When you say I should wear a business suit—is that where the jacket and pants match? I wore one thing for 30 years; I don't know what a suit is."

The importance of wardrobe should not be overlooked or understated. This can be a real challenge. If you have a support system that is informed about such things, you'll need to tap into it. Knowing what to wear and how to dress is not something we intuitively get; we all need to be shown.

In building your first wardrobe after the military, purchase foundational pieces first: a quality pair of slacks and blazer (for men and women) or even a business suit in a solid color (black, navy, or gray) give you many options. Buy the best you can afford and consider tailoring as part of your budget. A good tailor will make a less expensive suit look great because it is modified for your shape and size. Virtually all suits need tailoring.

Add a quality dress shirt in a nondistracting yet attractive color with a coordinating tie. A white dress shirt with a patterned tie is appropriate. Women should consider a blouse or top that doesn't distract from the look of the suit and is comfortable and good quality.

From there, add accessories. Men, investigate ties that reflect different feelings and looks. Women, add jewelry and belts to change up the look of the suit as desired.

Shoes and belts complete the look and should always be in coordinating colors and styles. Make sure they are well kept, polished, and free of any signs of excessive wear or damage.

Then you'll add slacks and skirts (women) and more pieces to your wardrobe as you have a sense of the kinds of roles you'll interview for and the companies you will pursue working for. Strive for quality over quantity and make sure the focus is on you, not on what you wear.

Start to Outline Your Resume

If you've never worked on your resume, it can feel daunting to list and catalog everything you've ever done in one document.

If you aren't sure what comes after the military for you, then list your experiences in bullet form, grouping together skills, expertise, decorations, and accomplishments. For now, just start capturing what you've done that will form the story you'll tell as you get closer to transition. Ignore formatting and templates at this point. Get the information onto paper.

Think about your resume as a reflection of what you've done before, highlighting the experiences, training, and skills that a future employer will be attracted to. Think strategically about your positioning going forward: What is most relevant to what you'll want to do next?

Write out your experiences in one section, listing your rank/title and the years you served in that role. Then move into the education you have today (and any commitments you've made along with anticipated graduation date). Create a section for skills and certifications and add any that come to mind.

Later in this book, I will show you more thoroughly how to craft your career-ready resume. For now, just capture ideas and words onto paper. If you know the civilian equivalent of the jobs you've done, great. If not, we'll get there.

Begin Building Your Online Profiles

Online tools will be an important part of your transition to the civilian workforce. Whether you use web portals to register for job fairs and apply for open positions or you use online tools to help build your personal brand, you'll want to get started before you depart your military career.

If you already have online profiles (such as LinkedIn, Facebook, Instagram, Twitter), review and update them following these guidelines:

- **Ensure you show up in a positive light.** If your Facebook timeline is packed with gruesome war images, for instance, consider the impression that will make with hiring managers. Remove anything from your profile that could be considered offensive, upsetting, or disrespectful to viewers.

- **Update your profiles with current information.** If you built your LinkedIn profile while in high school and haven't touched it since, it's time to add relevant, updated information. Your profile photo should look like you today. The skills, experience, and education sections should reflect where you are currently, even while you're still in uniform.

- **Evaluate your connections.** We are known by the company we keep, and online is no different. If your connections routinely post content that could be deemed offensive or upsetting, decide whether that's a connection you want to retain.

- **Start following companies.** If you are targeting certain industries or companies to explore for your next career, "follow" those companies on social networking sites, such as LinkedIn and Facebook. You'll begin learning about their corporate culture, trends, and issues that are important to them.

If you don't have any existing online profiles, then follow these steps to initiate your online presence now:

- **Create a LinkedIn profile.** LinkedIn focuses the conversation on professional topics, information, and issues instead of the more social or personal sites like Facebook. Set up a basic account, using your name as it appears on your resume. Upload a recent headshot into your profile, and add commentary about the kind of work you do and your experience. Be sure to include descriptions about your education and certifications. If LinkedIn recommends some "people you may know" and you're comfortable connecting with them, go ahead. Start building your network online.

- **Set up profiles on job sites, such as LinkedIn (jobs portal), Monster. com, or Indeed.com.** Your resume will come in handy for populating the experience sections of these sites. For now, strive to ensure each of your new profiles reflects the same person, using consistent language.

Talk to Your Support Network

As you move from what you know and whom you know into this next chapter in your career, the unknown can feel overwhelming, confusing, and frustrating. Be sure to talk to your spouse, family, friends, and peers about your transition, what you need and what they can expect.

Consider discussing with those people close to you:

- **What you are feeling.** Did you just turn in your separation papers and instantly have second thoughts? Do you regret not doing this sooner? Was there something that propelled you toward this decision—how does that feel? Feelings are natural and real, and they make us human. Your feelings are your own and they are right for you. You might be concerned because others seem to have their transition path clearly laid out and you worry that yours is less clearly defined. This is normal. You might feel like it's moving forward too easily—this was supposed to be hard, right?—and that can be normal for you. Just as no two people are the same, no two transitioning service members are the same. Share your feelings, concerns, joys, and questions with those close to you so they can best support you during this time.

- **What they can expect.** You will likely be immersed in the transition process, resources, and details, and your family will have questions. Whenever possible, engage your spouse in decision making and resources as you experience them. They are also going through a transition. Although there are robust programs to meet the needs of military spouses, in some cases it will feel better and be appropriate for your spouse to learn alongside you. In my workshops and trainings, I often have military spouses in the room, and it solidifies the learning for the service member.

- **What you will need.** It may be too early to know exactly what you'll need as you go through this process. Be open about that. As you get advice from your peers who've transitioned ahead of you, share those ideas with your spouse and support system so they can rely on best practices. You will need emotional support when things get frustrating or upsetting or require celebration; you'll need physical support for your relocation as well as your health; and you'll need spiritual support. You may also need financial support, depending on your situation and lifestyle.

   Gather your team and share, as best you can, what has worked for you in the past when you've made major life changes or had stress. Do you like talking through your stress, or do you prefer quiet reflection? Are you physical and appreciate a reassuring hug when you are upset, or could that upset you further? When and how should your support network voice their concern if they feel you aren't doing well?

- **How can you best support them?** Although your transition is about *your* next move, your family is a huge part of your life and career. Clarify their expectations and open the dialogue about what they need when they have questions or need reassurance. This builds a strong family foundation, which will be critical for a successful transition. Heather Ehle, founder of Project Sanctuary, a nonprofit organization helping military families, offers, "The most successful transitions happen when the service member involves the family and shifts their mindset to: 'who are my new battle buddies, and what is our new mission?' When the family is helping and supporting the service member, they feel like they are part of moving the family forward."

Create a Transition Timeline

After you hand in your separation papers, your transition officially begins. Hopefully you are thinking about the strategic steps to complete before you get to this stage, and now you're focused on what needs to happen to successfully launch your next path. The DoD suggests you begin planning for your retirement 24 months before leaving active duty. For those of you separating from active duty but not retiring, try to give yourself 18 months to plan.

Per the National Defense Authorization Act of FY19, beginning 1 October, all active duty members are required, by law, to complete mandatory Pre-Separation Counseling no less than 365 days from their separation/retirement date; Pre-Separation Counseling is a prerequisite for the TAP Workshop.

Prior to your Pre-Separation Counseling you will be required to attend one-on-one initial counseling, which, of course, backs up the timeline even more. Then you'll be required to complete your mandatory Capstone appointment no less than 120 days from your separation/retirement date, where you'll be asked to provide their career readiness standard deliverables (resume, budget, etc.).

Before you separate from your military duties, take the time to learn all you can about the process, requirements, opportunities, and challenges you might face. Learning about the differences between civilians and military personnel, the priorities of the business community, and how to best prepare yourself—strategically and tactically—will ready you for what comes next.

Transition Timeline

Consider this checklist of tasks to review and complete before you exit the military.

18 to 24 Months Out from Separation

- Complete your DD Form 2648, the DoD pre-separation counseling checklist to know which benefits and services you'll need counseling for.

- Review your military records to ensure they are accurate.

- Connect with your relocation and family readiness personnel on base to learn about available resources, and make an appointment with your local TAP counselor for your individualized counseling session. (These centers go by different names, based on your branch: Army Community Service Center, Airman & Family Readiness Center (Air Force), Fleet and Family Support Center (Navy), and Marine and Family Services.)

- Complete your Individual Transition Plan (with your counselor).

- If retiring or separating, schedule and attend pre-separation counseling no later than 365 days out.

- Register for TAP classes.

- Secure your Joint Service Transcript or Community College of the Air Force transcript and Verification of Military Experience and Training.

- Talk to your family about their goals and needs immediately after your separation and long term.

- Identify any extenuating family issues that will impact or direct your career and location options.

- Decide whether you'll pursue a different type of work, and if so, what that will look like.

- Determine your financial goals after separation—how much will you need to earn? What additional benefits (healthcare, financial, housing, education, etc.) will you and your family need?

- Decide whether you'll be launching a new business or pursuing school after separation. Begin sketching that out now.

- List and gather any licenses, specialized training certificates, diplomas, and technical training you've received.

- List any prior civilian work experience you had before joining the military.

- Start building social media profiles, beginning with a LinkedIn profile. A simple LinkedIn profile will suffice for now, but you'll want to build it out shortly.

- Research where you might want to live and work, evaluating options for the kind of work you are interested in and companies based there. For instance, you might want to live in Oahu, Hawaii, because you love to surf, but options for your type of work might not be available there.

- Work on reframing your thinking around the civilian sector. Dispel biases or misperceptions you have about what it will be like to work alongside nonmilitary individuals and frame your thinking to be open-minded and optimistic.

6 to 12 Months Out from Separation

- Find a secure place to store your DD-214, recognizing how important this document is to your transition.

- If you haven't already, register and attend TAP classes.

- Complete your Military Occupational Code Crosswalk and Gap Analysis.

- Explore and understand y our Veterans Affairs benefits and services (register on eBenefits to learn more).

- If you haven't already, create a skeletal resume—list what you've done and the results you've achieved. Wherever you can, consider the civilian equivalent of the work you've done, and migrate your resume into language that a civilian hiring manager in your targeted industry will understand.

- Then begin modifying your resume to suit the requirements of positions you might start applying to.

- Create a list of target companies. Who's your dream employer?

- Explore options for internships or apprenticeships through DOD SkillBridge, fellowships through Hire Our Heroes, or other programs. Apply to those that you qualify for, and where your post-military career will benefit. Investigate whether internships, fellowships, and apprenticeships would be helpful to give you advantage or insight when you enter the civilian sector.

- Find a mentor or coach who can help guide you through transition. Initiate those conversations now.

- Begin informational interviews with contacts who can provide insight into companies, industries, and opportunities.

- Start planning your post-military career wardrobe. Research what you'll need to buy for job interviews, networking meetings, attending job fairs, and so on.

- Sign up for your free one-year premium membership on LinkedIn.

- Start taking LinkedIn Learning courses in your area of interest or where you could benefit from learning the content.

- Join groups or associations around your industry target, hobbies, or interests. Consider attending meetings of chambers of commerce, Toastmasters, and local job searching groups to better learn the language and needs of employers in those areas.

3 Months Out from Separation

- Complete all mandatory Department of Labor employment fundamentals for career transition, regardless of whether you choose the employment, education, or vocational training tracks.

- Consider whether to take terminal leave or sell back your leave balance.

- Schedule your Capstone event with your commander or their designee.

- Begin crafting your elevator pitch—how you'll answer the "tell me about yourself" question.

- Start attending job fairs and career expos in your area and your industry. Use the strategies I describe in Chapter 6.

- Refine your social media profiles to clarify what you're looking to do next and what you can offer.

- Refine your resume now that you've done some research and had some conversations. If you've worked in an internship, catalog your activities and any achievements and work them into the resume.

- Begin reaching out to your network for post-military conversations and face-to-face meetings. Networking is crucial at this point.

- You may already be applying for jobs and interviewing at this time. Be sure to track each resume sent, follow up, and stay in touch with the employer even if you aren't selected for hire.

- Let employers you interview with know of your available start date. If you'll be relocating, indicate a preference for phone and video interviews first.

30 Days Out from Separation

- Intensify your informational interviews—get more specific about what you're looking to learn from the people you interview. Look for patterns in the information they share. What are they suggesting that will help you be successful?

- Continue inviting people to connect on LinkedIn—send personalized introductions with your request. Accept connections from people with whom you would benefit from knowing.

- Refine your resume, targeting the industries, companies, and type of work you'll pursue.

- Check in with yourself. How are you feeling? What concerns or questions are rising up? Talk to your peers or mentor about these feelings, and get guidance for managing these natural emotions.

- Set meetings and appointments for after you relocate. This will help you integrate into your new community, familiarize yourself with the business community where you'll work, and start your network of professional contacts.

1 Week Out from Separation

- Relax. Yes, I said relax. The stress of separation, relocation, and a new career can feel overwhelming. Give yourself time to catch up on sleep, be (or get) healthy, and connect with family and friends. Take this time to take care of yourself, and you'll be in better shape and condition to resume your transition after separation.

- If you have a job to move to, resist starting the week following your retirement or separation. Give yourself a week or longer to acclimate to your new surroundings and life.

- Set meetings and appointments for the following weeks if you haven't already done this.

- Pick a date when you'll hit the job search hard. Pick a date when your job search will commence in full force (if you haven't already begun).

In Closing

Several years ago, I had the opportunity to coach a group of special operations personnel transitioning to various corporate jobs after the military. In my group I had Army Rangers, Green Berets, and Navy SEALs. Our training was proceeding well as I introduced them to the concept of personal branding, highlighted realities of the military-to-civilian divide, and walked them through creation of a career road-map and timeline.

That's when one of the SEALs stopped me and remarked, "Ma'am, you need to understand something. While we're in uniform, we are trained for the most high-risk, unconventional warfare imaginable. You could drop us out of any plane, truck, boat, helicopter in any part of the world, and we know how to successfully complete the mission. But this... what you're talking about in asking us who we are, what we're passionate about and who we want to be when we take the uniform off, getting into a new career and being able to support ourselves and our families. This is terrifying." He shared that they were feeling unprepared for the next chapter of their lives because they lacked the training and tools to be successful.

Your life after the military starts the day you enter the military. Planning for what comes next should begin early and should be maintained until the last day you drive off the base.

By understanding the culture and community of the people you will work alongside in the civilian sector, you can prepare yourself to recognize the differences and appreciate the similarities.

Start building your online assets and career tools, and you'll be in a more empowered position to take advantage of the plethora of career transition and readiness tools available to you through your branch of service and through the DoD's transition program.

The tools provided here and in the rest of this book will give you a solid place to start from and build off of as you navigate your career after military service.

Evaluating the Path Forward 03

Employment, Education, or Entrepreneurship

Your recruiter told you that after your time in the military everything would be OK. It's a lie. You have to do the work.

—Retired Army recruiter

In the midst of the stress over "what to do next?," you may rush to secure a post-military job in the hope that having a job will calm your fears and anxiety about life after service. As best you can, resist this temptation and look at your career options as a whole. Chris Sanchez, a retired Navy SEAL shares, "If you don't figure out what you want to do first, you may find yourself making suboptimal job choices, job hopping, or displaying a lack of confidence in interviews."

For many of you, work and income are necessary to provide for your family. As you consider whether to seek employment, pursue advanced education, or follow the path to self-employment and entrepreneurship, a number of factors will impact your decision: your personal passion, values, family goals, medical needs, desired location, financial needs and goals, and career aspirations.

Finding Your Passion

Just Because You Want to Doesn't Mean You Can

Desire and ability sometimes don't line up. Whether your limitations come from geography (there aren't companies in the town you want to live in that offer the kind of work you'd love to do) or because of physical limitations (perhaps you're too old to play in the NFL) or because of family obligations, or skills or abilities, sometimes your goals aren't realistic or practical.

At the same time, it's important not to give up on a dream too early. Before you decide against pursuing your passion, explore all available options. Are you not able to sell your artwork because you live in a remote rural community? Consider promoting and selling your work online. If your dream of being a mental health counselor is stunted by your lack of education and need to provide income for your family, consider night school. Don't put the dream away because of limitations that can be overcome, but be realistic about the possibilities and options.

Just Because You Can Doesn't Mean You Should

A few years ago, I coached a young man who was being medically discharged from the Army. He was leaving his military career many years before he anticipated and had not prepared for a life and career out of uniform. He was admittedly overwhelmed with decisions.

Each time I asked him about potential jobs and careers he might pursue, he'd reply with "Yeah, I could do that." It seemed his choices were limitless.

But I knew that there were some things he'd want to do that he wouldn't be able to do (for health reasons). I also knew there were things he would be qualified to do, or would know how to do, but wouldn't want to do. I call this the "just because you can, doesn't mean you should" rule.

We discussed jobs he would hate to do. I asked him to list any occupation he thought sounded horrible. He started with "the guy that cleans up after the zoo animals" and ended with "working in a cubicle all day in a call center, talking to angry customers."

As important as it is to dream about a career that excites you, it's equally important to be clear about what you *don't* want. If the thought of sitting behind a desk, answering upset customer calls, and reading from a script of responses doesn't excite you, that's OK! By recognizing this, you're one step closer to discovering what you want to do.

Using the call center example, be specific about which aspects of the work are really unappealing to you. Is it the fact that you'd be indoors and not outside? Do you despise talking on the phone? Or do you not like the idea of reading a set of scripted responses?

At first pass, this exercise may lead you to believe that you shouldn't pursue any job that requires desk time, or phone time, or customer communication, but I'd suggest taking another pass with a more nuanced approach. Rather than eliminating an entire class of jobs, push yourself to get specific about what exactly doesn't appeal to you while also reflecting on what aspects of the job might suit you well. For instance, if you worked at a desk and engaged with customers who came to see you and needed your advice or help, would that be more attractive? If so, it's important to recognize that while you are uncomfortable serving angry people through a phone line, you actually might enjoy interacting with people in a helpful way. This realization can help you find a role that best suits you.

Career Nonnegotiables

Similar to your passions, it's critical that you identify your nonnegotiables. These are the deal breakers you won't do, tolerate, or accept going forward. As you reflect on nonnegotiables—what you won't tolerate—ask yourself these questions:

- Which of my values could I not adjust on the job? For instance, if honesty is a foundation of who I am and what I believe in, could I work for a company that lied to its customers in the past?

- Do I need to work only with people who believe what I believe, who value the same things I do? Which beliefs and values are so critical for me that I can't deviate from them?

- Could I work within a culture that had differing values, in the hopes I could influence those values?

What Are Your Must-Haves?

Picture yourself working in a civilian company. What nonnegotiables would stop you from accepting a position in the first place or could cause you to leave a company? Consider:

- Is title important to me? If so, why? Would I be flexible on title and responsibilities for the right position?

- How quickly would I want to be promoted? Recognizing that advancement in civilian workplace is not as predictable as it is in the military, what's my timeline?

- What about the nature of the company's industry or business? Are there businesses, industries, or companies whose work I could not get behind and support?

- What culture and work style suit me best? Are there work styles I would find difficult to manage through? Could I work alongside creative, expressive, and outgoing people, or would I need to work in a quiet, more introspective and reserved environment?

Family and Lifestyle Nonnegotiables

Your next career may require you to ramp up your skills, training, network, and experience. While in the military, you became accustomed to PCSing, relocating your family and reestablishing where "home" was temporarily and often. Consider the impact on your family and lifestyle after the service through a similar lens by asking yourself:

- Will I allow for some travel in my next career? How much is acceptable?

- Is it critical that I am near medical or rehabilitation resources? Which ones? Are those located near my desired geography?

- Have I picked the city where I'll live with my family? What career options or limitations does that afford me?

- Will I work an 80-hour week? If not, how much time will I dedicate to my job?

- Is working weekends and evenings acceptable to me and my family?

Financial Nonnegotiables

Finally, what will you and your family need to live on? This is not the same question as "What would you like to earn?" or even "What do you believe you deserve to earn?" Many retiring service members believe their commitment and duty to country means they have earned the right to a higher pay and deserve to be rewarded for their time away from family and civilian work. This is a difficult position to hold.

Employers care about what you need to feed your family, to a point. If you purchased an expensive home, put your children in private schools, and bought a luxury automobile, that doesn't mean the employer needs to pay you more. Employers have a set budget based on established requirements and goals for each open position.

Be very clear about your financial goals and needs. How low of a salary could you accept and still provide for your family? That may be one end of your scale. On the other end of the scale is what you'd like to earn, based on your experience, expertise, value-add, and what the market pays for that work. Somewhere in between is what you might accept.

Using Assessments

It may be helpful to assess your skills and talents to understand which fields are most interesting and viable for you. You might use an online or in-person career assessment tool similar to the aptitude test you're given in the military as you prepare to separate in order to match your strengths, personal qualities, preferences, and talents with career options. Online quizzes and assessments can also help you understand your preferences, blind spots, and options.

Weighing Your Options

After considering all of these factors, remember that you can—and likely will—pivot during your career at least a few times. You may graduate from school and get a job or become an entrepreneur. Or you may start with a job and realize that more schooling would make you a stronger contributor. Your passion for entrepreneurship may start with a job in a similar company, where you learn about business, hiring, strategy, marketing, and so on. The point is, the options you're evaluating now do not have to be permanent. They are just your starting point upon leaving the military.

The Employment Path

Employment after the military can take several paths. You could work in the government sector, for a nonprofit organization, a for-profit company, or a start-up venture. You could work for a very large company with hundreds of thousands of employees around the globe or you could work for a small, entrepreneurial company that employs just a handful of employees. In the employment sector, businesses and organizations have varied sizes, formats, processes, or cultures.

Considering employment should mean evaluating your nonnegotiables, your dreams and goals, and then seeing which industry or company aligns with your vision, values, and skills. Companies of all sizes and structures have values—some are well publicized and promoted while others are more discreet. Not all of those company values will align with your own.

If you are considering public or private sector employment, ask yourself:

- How's the job market?
- Are you looking for work similar to what you did in the military?
- Is there demand for your skills and experience?
- If you are changing jobs completely, what skills, training, or education will you need?
- At what level can you enter a company—entry level, management, senior leadership?

Let's look at a few examples of military-to-civilian transition and how the path to employment was tied to vision and values for these veterans.

CASE STUDY   Doug Bartels, from Fighter Pilot to Finance

For as long as he could remember, Doug Bartels (USAF) wanted to be a fighter pilot—and not just any fighter pilot, he wanted to fly the coveted F-15E Strike Eagle as a combat aviator. After graduating with a Bachelor of Science degree from the US Air Force Academy, he was chosen for pilot training and eventually was selected to serve as a Strike Eagle pilot, fulfilling his childhood dream.

However, when balancing the needs of his family with the demands of an Air Force career became too great, Bartels decided to leave the Air Force after a 12-year active duty career. "Flying F-15Es was my identity." He notes, "I completed multiple combat deployments, graduated from Fighter Weapons School (i.e., Top Gun), and had an assignment as a test pilot in Nevada."

After leaving the military, he could have easily transferred his skills into becoming a commercial airline pilot. Instead, Bartels decided to go back to school and was accepted into the MBA program at Duke University.

After graduation, he set out to make money on Wall Street. In 2007, Bartels entered the financial services world. Given his military training and an MBA from Duke, he believed his future was clear and bright.

Unfortunately, the markets collapsed in 2008, and Bartels watched many financial services firms close, downsize, or scramble to remain solvent. His "safe path" to career stability turned out to be a very rocky road.

When his wife received a job offer and relocation package to Las Vegas, where he had once served while on active duty, the family moved. Bartels made a lateral move to a smaller financial services firm in California and joined the Air Force Reserves. The choice was a hard one: He thought that he had closed the door on his military lifestyle and mindset, but now he was jumping back into the same structure, processes, culture, and systems he'd left a few years earlier.

What was even more challenging was that the only job available for him was manning drones as an MQ-9 operator. He accepted the role because of the economic instability he experienced, and he feared not being able to provide for his family. Also, having completed 12 years of active duty, he could receive a reserve retirement after eight more years of service, which appealed to him.

Although initially his decision to join the Reserves was a financial one, Bartels later realized it connected him with like-minded individuals who were loyal to the military and also building civilian careers. Joining the Reserves also provided him with the opportunity to mentor and coach other service members. In the end, what started as a career move born out of necessity became a life-changing and positive choice.

Bartels rebounded from this initial career setback and is thriving in his current role as a corporate strategy executive with a global industrial conglomerate. "I learned to check myself and my ego after leaving the military. What worked when I was in uniform didn't bring me the same benefits in the civilian sector. Reinventing my career took a lot of humility, patience, and unexpected turns. But I had good coaches and mentors to guide me forward."

Looking back, Bartels admits there were lessons he wished he'd learned sooner or better. For transitioning veterans, he advises:

1 **Take the time to understand yourself and your values.** "Just like we did as fighter pilots, you have to know who you are and what you're capable of before you're tested." Bartels encourages veterans to get clear on who they are, what they're good at, what they stand for, and what they truly want before they move to their next career. "If you can't do this yourself, get a mentor or talk to someone you trust who can provide you with an unbiased external perspective."

2 **Develop a detailed action plan and account for uncertainty.** Visualize what the future can be and run all options in your mind. "I remember being a mission commander and sitting in my tent the night before a combat mission. I'd visualize the entire mission as best as I could—picturing every radio call, aircraft movement, and enemy actions—and how I'd respond." Bottom line: Set your aim on what you want, build a detailed plan, and consider as many what-ifs as possible that could derail you from achieving your aim.

3 **Execute the plan and don't look back.** Make each step intentional and learn to get comfortable with discomfort and uncertainty. There will be times you'll find success and joy, and many others where you'll be frustrated and scared. That's all part of the process. Find the mental awareness, fortitude, and grit to work through discomfort—after all, that's what every veteran learns during their military service!

CASE STUDY   Dave Bradt, from Combat to Corporate

Dave Bradt recognizes that when he left the Marine Corps, he likely had more leadership training and experience than most people his age. While in uniform, he earned a master's degree and served in highly combat-centric missions, seeing direct combat and combat support.

As a captain, he was told that he would have many options upon leaving the military. "'The world is your oyster,' people told me," says Bradt. And while he expected his work in the civilian sector would be different, he quickly realized how different his new peers, and the organizational cultures, were.

"The culture of combat back in the 2004–2011 time frame was predominantly male, very intense, and distinctly challenging," Bradt says. "The mindset and behaviors that we, in a combat unit, adopt to be successful are long lasting. They don't just disappear post-deployment. To thrive in a noncombat environment, you must transition away from that mindset and those associated behaviors, or at least the ones that aren't serving you well."

After two deployments to the war in Iraq, serving as a Combat Engineer Platoon Commander attached to a Marine Infantry Battalion responsible for weapons cache reconnaissance and demolitions work and a subsequent tour of duty in Washington, DC, as the executive officer of a counter-IED task force, Bradt felt it was time for a change. He left the Marines and set out to join the civilian sector.

His work in counterintelligence, large-scale combat, and construction made him attractive to large consulting firms who worked with defense agencies. Soon after leaving the military, Bradt was recruited by a large Fortune 100 consulting firm where he'd focus on helping defense, military, and other clients grow their organizations. He accepted the job because it made sense to get more widespread and general real-world business experience with a well-established, large firm, which he believed would provide him many opportunities to grow. But he quickly grew unsatisfied.

"I missed the front lines: the stress, adrenaline, importance of my work," Bradt explains. "There's something to be said for the warrior ethos of the military. The Marine Corps, like all military branches, has more than its fair share of rules and processes, but the camaraderie and purpose to something bigger than oneself are what many veterans miss in Corporate America," he adds.

Bradt ended up leaving the consulting firm to pursue a career path that would leverage his leadership and resiliency skills. His ability to lead large teams could help organizations see options where they only saw challenges, and he could choose to work for a company whose values aligned with his own. He found it in a large company in the entertainment industry.

In his current role, he helps internal organizations grow and learn. He works fast and with a furious passion for excellence. He understands the rules of engagement, can succeed within the company culture and systems for growth, and feels that he gets to be himself at work.

Bradt realized he needed to start by looking at what he wanted to do, not just what he was qualified to do. His frontline training qualified him to serve companies in a consulting role where the stakes might not be the same (not life and death) but the impact is significant. He thrives in situations where he's given some autonomy yet has team interaction periodically.

Bradt's advice to veterans with unique, seemingly nontransferrable military experience includes:

1 **If you can, take time off after your military commitment to find yourself and disconnect from the service.** Travel, spend time with family, connect with your community, find a new community. If you jump into the first thing offered because you're nervous about being unemployed, you can actually delay finding what makes you truly happy.

2 **Take risks.** Listen to your heart and let yourself get uncomfortable. This transition will feel like nothing you've ever done before—you'll feel highs and lows that no training can prepare you for. Breathe through those times and don't be afraid to try something new.

3 **Resist talking constantly about your military experience after you leave.** Civilians can't understand what you've done or been through—they weren't there. You'll confuse your supervisors and peers if you relate everything in your life to your time in the military.

The Path to Entrepreneurship

Did you know that many well-known American companies were founded by military veterans? Nike, Walmart, RE/MAX, FedEx, GoDaddy, Sports Clips, and Sperry Shoes are some of the businesses founded by military veterans that have grown to international significance. Does the idea of forging your own path appeal to you?

The desire to start your own company, be your own boss, and control your own destiny can be very appealing after years in military service.

Perhaps you can't imagine working for someone else and will figure out a business after you exit the military, or maybe you've had a business idea for years and finally feel ready to pull the plug and get going. Either way, being a business owner is a compelling path for many.

Yet it is important to recognize that the entrepreneurial path is not linear and is paved with challenges as well as opportunities. If you wish to pursue a career as an entrepreneur, ask yourself:

- Are you in a good position (financially, emotionally, physically) to start your own business?
- Do you have a business plan?
- Where is your passion coming from for this venture?
- What does the market look like for your business, product, or service?
- Do you have advisors and mentors who can help you?

Ask anyone who's started, grown, and scaled a company how they did it, and they'll share various options and strategies that worked for them (but might not work for you).

Should You Consider a Franchise?

When you see the word "franchise," do you imagine fast food service, spending a lot of money to get into the franchise, or needing a lot of industry knowledge before you can successfully run a franchise operation? Unfortunately, these ideas keep many veterans from building their career as a franchisee.

Susan Scotts, a career transition coach who helps veterans pursue business ownership through franchising, explains that there are more than 3,000 franchise brands in the United States today, spanning 85 different industries (only 10 percent of franchises are food related). Franchises can even be home-based, smaller in scope, or service based. The variety of franchise formats provides opportunities for veterans who are in school now but want a side business that can become a full-time job after graduation. According to Scotts, some franchise models can be successfully worked part-time.

Scotts advises veterans to consider several things as they pursue entrepreneurship and consider franchising:

1 **Consider what you enjoy doing.** There are likely franchise models available to support your hobbies and interests.

2 **What's your background?** If you worked in operations in the Army, you likely have the skills to run a franchise. A recruiter in the Marines? You'd enjoy the social and community aspects of franchise ownership.

3 **Recognize that there are discounts, programs, and incentives for veterans to enter franchising.** In some cases, veterans receive substantial discounts on the initial investment. The US Small Business Administration offers special funding for veterans who have good credit and requires no pledge of collateral. You can use this funding to pay yourself a salary, to offset the initial franchise investment, and for working capital.

Franchising requires discipline, commitment, and a passion for business ownership. After investigating options, speak to other veterans to learn best practices.

Choosing Entrepreneurship

Here are stories of two veterans who felt the call to entrepreneurship. Although your situation may be different in some ways, it is useful to understand how they approached their solo ventures in order to help you decide whether entrepreneurship is the right path for you.

CASE STUDY   Jan Rutherford, from Green Beret to Leadership Coach

"The thing I kept telling myself, early in building my own company, was 'Why didn't I start this sooner?'" says Jan Rutherford, a former Army medic and Green Beret, who left the military in his 20s and set out to learn all he needed to learn to become a successful entrepreneur. When he states how much he wishes he'd started earlier, Rutherford's wife reminds him, "You weren't ready. There was so much you needed to do and learn before you could lead others the way you lead now."

From an early age, Rutherford knew he wanted to be an entrepreneur and to be an executive in a big company. He also knew that corporate experience would set him up for entrepreneurial success.

He joined the Army two weeks after graduating high school and at 19 years of age was awarded the Green Beret. Shortly thereafter, he was tapped to be an instructor, teaching and leading others in the Special Forces. During his years in the Army, Rutherford learned how to serve, lead, collaborate, and drive progress in a structured, predictable environment.

His career in corporate America began just before his 27th birthday with a prominent and growing pharmaceutical company. What attracted him to this company is that they promoted and lived two values at every level of the organization.

1 Those who produce will share in the result.

2 Treat others the way you'd like to be treated.

These values shaped his leadership beliefs.

After growing his skills, passion, and talents first in the Army and then for ten years at the company, Rutherford realized his goal was to train and develop people to lead.

After a brief stint at a healthcare IT company as the turnaround CEO, Jan started his own company focused on one thing: helping selfless, adventurous leaders who have heroic aspirations beyond power and money succeed. Among other things, his company provides experiential training in challenging conditions for senior business executives and Special Operations veterans in transition. The executives learn how to slow down, detox from their daily lives and stress, and focus on priorities and purposefulness. The veterans learn essential skills needed for a successful transition into the business arena.

After his military career, Rutherford knew he wanted to be an entrepreneur but realized he needed to gain some corporate experience before setting out on his own. His advice to other entrepreneurs is:

1 **Consider your values carefully.** Get real on what you hold dear. Prioritize them or your values will compete and impact your ability to be successful.

2 **Get clear on what you really want.** Rutherford suggests you ask yourself, "For whose good do you serve?" Who are your people and where are they now? What can you do for them that's valuable and important?

3 **What skills and experiences do you need to get to your dream?** Study, meet, shadow, and interview people who are doing the work you want to do. Don't talk to CEOs if you want to be a project manager. Talk to the best project managers out there.

CASE STUDY   Kristina Guerrero, From Combat Pilot to Dog Snacks

When Kristina Guerrero exited the US Air Force in 2010 as a pilot captain of the C-130 TurboPROPS in several combat missions in both Iraq and Afghanistan, she pursued a career as an occupational therapist. She envisioned this job would be steady and interesting work and could combine her love of health and people in a meaningful way.

But in 2011, on a nature hike with her dog, she got the idea to create a company offering healthy and compact dog snacks (grain-free, all-natural full meals in a small size). Her passion for health would now be in service to dogs, her other love. Using her own savings and relying on seemingly unrelated skills developed in the military, Guerrero launched her company, TurboPUP.

TurboPUP fit a niche in the market—pet owners who wanted a healthy solution to an active lifestyle with their dogs. With help and insights from friends and programs that foster veteran entrepreneurship, Guerrero's company grew. In 2014, she auditioned for and in early 2015 she appeared on the popular network television show *Shark Tank*. *Shark Tank* features prominent, successful investors who evaluate pitches from entrepreneurs and inventors. If and when the investors pursue an opportunity, they typically offer financial investment, coaching, mentoring, and other resources to help the entrepreneur or inventor succeed.

During her business pitch on *Shark Tank*, Guerrero talked about her military career, her passion for business ownership, and the business of TurboPUP. She wanted to grow the company but needed the resources and talents of these expert entrepreneurs to get there. One shark "bit," and her company received capital, valuable insight, and mentoring.

Outside of the valuable resources she received from the *Shark Tank* investor, Guerrero credits her military training with much of her growth and success. She realized she needed to depend on others to be successful, so she reached out for help and outsourced some of the work. She also drew on her military background to mitigate risk and exposure while at the same time leveraging promotions and public relations to gain visibility for the product with target consumers. And she channeled her skills as a pilot to become a focused and committed business owner. With help from her *Shark Tank* coach and encouragement from her family, Guerrero grew the TurboPUP business.

Guerrero learned many lessons as she grew her venture and encourages other veterans-turned-entrepreneurs to consider these tips:

1 **Remember how to execute on a mission.** In the military, you're trained to carry a lot of responsibility, often at a very young age, and to use what you know to successfully complete whatever mission you're given. Whether you're flying in a combat mission or starting a company, identify all the steps and resources you'll need to be successful.

   For example, in order to successfully fly a mission, you need to consider fuel loads, intel, air traffic control considerations, and more. When you start a company, you also have to think of the pieces and systems you'll need, such as lawyers, bankers, accountants, manufacturers, distribution options, marketing plans, and employees.

2 **Rely on your resiliency and problem-solving skills.** As with any mission in combat, you can prepare and plan, but in the actual moment, things come up. You're trained to navigate them and complete the mission. Similarly, as a business owner, you have to plan for distribution challenges, inventory slowdowns, marketing glitches, and staff changes. Veterans know how to problem solve through challenges. As a business owner, the challenges look different, but you can use a similar approach to find a solution. Rely on the muscle memory of what you learned in the military.

3 **Leverage all of your skills, even your people skills.** The leadership and communication style of the military might look different from a civilian environment, but your skills as a veteran are relevant. "When I was in uniform," Kristina notes, "my skills were matched by the others who did the same job as me. When I became a business owner, I realized just how unique and valuable my skills and training really was."

As a veteran, you know management. You know leadership and stress and risk. The skills you developed in the military will serve you with patience, under-standing, compassion, and discipline as a business owner and entrepreneur.

The Post-Military Path to Education

Deciding to go back to school after military service is not an easy choice for some. You know you'll be postponing your income-earning days, you will be older than the more traditional college student, and you may need to modify your lifestyle to live on GI Bill stipends. But the opportunities and potential for your life and career gained through a college or graduate school experience are exponential, and for many of you this will be the best choice.

If you are considering education as your path, ask yourself:

- Can you afford to go to school full time?
- Will you need to work while going to school?
- Is there a market for the kind of job you'll have after school?
- Can you get into your first-choice school? What about second choice?
- Are there other needs you'll have to attend to while you're in school (i.e., medical, child care)?

Once you decide to go back to school, your next choice will be what to study and where to attend. Nearly every college and university in the United States has programs for student veterans, which is great news for veterans pursuing education. Transitioning veterans will find resources, peers with similar experiences, and a sense of support and community on campus that may not have been there 10 or 15 years ago.

The goal of school is to level up your skills, expertise, and talents to make you more informed, knowledgeable, and valuable in your next career. The path you take—Bachelor of Arts? Bachelor of Science? Graduate degree in biochemistry or master's in business administration (MBA)?—should stem from your passion, talents, and overall career aspirations.

CASE STUDY   Sean Brown, from Veteran to Student to Employee

When Sean Brown left the Marine Corps infantry in 2010, he wasn't sure what to do next. He had a strong passion to serve and figured the police department would leverage his military training and provide a similar work environment to what he knew in the Marines.

He relocated home to Las Vegas, Nevada, with hopes of joining the police force there. Shortly after getting settled, however, local police resources were redistributed, causing a hiring freeze to be put in place.

Brown saw education as a way to gain greater options: He researched the markets that were hiring where his skills and passions would be valuable and enrolled in a mechanical engineering program to begin his Plan B career.

Through an internship with a large defense contractor, Brown learned that his skills needed to broaden even further. The company asked him to pursue a path in electrical engineering—where its needs were greater—and when Brown complied, the company was impressed with his resiliency and positive attitude. He was offered a great job opportunity after his internship ended, and the company paid for his relocation to their office in another state.

Although school offered many educational benefits, Brown also credits his success to his involvement on campus as a student veteran. He joined the Student Veterans of America chapter on campus (later becoming the chapter president) and mentored other student veterans on the ins and outs of being a nontraditional student.

Brown advises other student veterans to:

1 **Get involved in an organization on campus.** Your mental state and outlook will be different because you are not entering college or graduate school through a traditional path. This is OK. Surround yourself with like-minded people where you can learn from each other.

2 **Connect with your veteran center on campus.** The counselors there will provide you with lists to help guide you through schooling and accessing your benefits as a veteran.

3 **Speak to an academic advisor in the department you're interested in.** Ask about internships and career opportunities. Discuss whether you can pursue additional certifications while you're in school (e.g., can you get your Professional Engineer Certification as you pursue your engineering degree?)

4 **Join study groups, labs, partner groups, and committees that are all focused on the same mission: graduation.**

5 **Find a degree program that leads to a career, not just a degree in something that feels easy to you.** "I saw that jobs in STEM were growing and not slowing down. There's a career path there that would last me many years," notes Brown.

6 **Attend job fairs, conferences, and career expos on campus.** You'll meet employers, learn of internships, and broaden your view of what's available after graduation.

7 **Keep your resume and LinkedIn profile updated at all times.** You might be in an internship and get asked for your resume because the company wants to start the hiring process early. Be ready!

In Closing

No two veterans have the exact same transition out of the military. The person sitting to the right of you will have challenges and opportunities you can't imagine. The person to the left of you might find a job right out of the military... and be back in the job search in six months. It takes a lot of work to prepare yourself for this transition. You have to anticipate and consider as many variables as possible, examine your goals, inventory your skills and abilities, consider your options going forward (including employment, entrepreneurship, and education), weigh your nonnegotiables, and take the first step toward this new chapter in your life. You will learn lessons and likely course-correct along the way. All of this is normal and expected. It all starts with planning, preparation, and action.

Building Your Personal Brand 04

Almost without fail, when I begin to speak at a military job fair, on a base, or to a classroom of transitioning service members and I say the words "personal branding," eyes roll. I've been told that those words conjure images of self-aggrandizement, boasting, and arrogant behavior in the minds of active duty service members and veterans, and it is highly unpleasant.

Personal branding is anything but arrogance and bragging. It is a skill and habit you will find crucial to career success out of uniform. As you move through this chapter, we'll discuss what a personal brand is and why it will become a critical tool in your transition toolkit, how to build and grow your brand, and various ways to apply and measure the effectiveness of your personal brand in creating and driving your post-military reputation.

Understanding Personal Brand

What Is a Personal Brand?

Essentially, your personal brand is your consciously designed impression to the world—employers, colleagues, and the like—of what they can expect from you. With and through your personal brand (internal), you direct others to create a perception of who you are and what you value. The perception in other people's minds of you forms your reputation (external). As you shape and build your personal brand, you guide people's perception of you to ensure they recognize and value you for the skills, character traits, beliefs, and goals you set.

When we hear "brand," we often think of logos or consumer products like Nike or Coca-Cola or BMW. Those companies and their products set an expectation in our minds of what they stand for and the value we'll derive if we engage (buy) their products. For example, if I want to buy a BMW, I believe I'll get status and prestige by owning one. People will view me as more attractive, successful, and powerful if I drive up in a BMW. This is perception and belief based.

Brands live in beliefs, feelings, and perception. When companies like BMW create a brand, they are very clear about the feelings they want to conjure up in the minds of their target audience. Then the marketing team takes those desired feelings and creates marketing and advertising campaigns to communicate with their target audience, hopefully resulting in a sale.

Your personal brand works the same way and also lives in the feelings and beliefs you set. Your brand drives your reputation—who you are, how you show up, and what you are passionate about. I describe your personal brand as the operating principle through which all decisions are made because, as you will see, your brand lives through your values. Without values, brands are vapid and unsustainable, but when lived through values, personal brands can be authentic, meaningful, and sustainable.

Your personal brand represents the "who" (Who am I?), the "how" (How am I relevant and compelling?) and, most important, the "why" (Why do I care? Why am I here? Why should we work together/know each other?)

In my 2016 TEDx Talk about my work with military veterans titled *The Power of Gratitude and Generosity—Serving Those Who Have Served*, I shared a quote attributed to Mark Twain: "There are two important days in your life: The day you were born, and the day you find out why." (To access my Talk, please go to www.youtube.com/watch?v= 9BloWnsJCRw&feature=youtu.be). Your personal brand helps you discover why you are here and how you are meant to serve. For most of you, service is part of who you are—and may have been a huge driver in your decision to join the military. Your "purpose" going forward, out of the military, can still be to serve. Through the process of self-discovery in clarifying your personal brand, you'll uncover your purpose and build systems to ensure you position yourself consistently with your values and goals.

Why Personal Branding Matters

As I wrote about in my 2014 book, *Your Next Mission: A Personal Branding Guide for the Military-to-Civilian Transition*:

> Judgment and perception are part of our lives as humans. We instinctively judge other people—it's our nature. We form opinions about people based on how they act, what they look like, how they sound and how we feel about them. And that judgment is important as a survival skill—on the battlefield and in business.
>
> [A]s you undoubtedly experienced in your military training, being able to "size up" the enemy or a potential opponent is critical to your survival, the protection of your fellow troops, and the success of your mission. Whether you serve at 30,000 feet or on the ground, in military service you learned to form opinions that would advance your situation and positioning strategically. In a civilian environment, you will also need to judge things like whether your colleagues can keep information confidential, if you can rely on them to meet goals and expectations, and whether you want to bring them on an important sales call.

Personal branding matters today more than ever before. When Randall Niznick exited the Navy after 23 years, he thought his experience was a shoo-in for his dream job in facilities management. He quickly learned that his many years of facilities operations management experience and his multiple-year tour with the Department of State managing security systems only got him so far.

"After struggling to find my ideal job out of the Navy, I found Lida Citroën's work on personal branding and realized I was missing an established brand," Niznick remembers. "For many (including me), it was easy to have our military uniform and/or rank be our brand. I was a Chief in the Navy and being 'the chief' comes with a certain cachet that is well known in the military services."

Niznick created a personal branding statement—"I serve people and communities through sustainable facilities management"—and set out to market himself. He shared his brand with connections on LinkedIn and in person, and soon opportunities presented themselves. "Through all those opportunities I kept defining who I truly was... it was always evolving because I had to lose my 'I was a chief' mentality, which is not easy to do," Niznick shared.

When we manage and craft our personal brands, we are in control of the narrative around who we are and what we can offer. The randomness and ambiguity around why we are here and what we can do dissipates. Instead, those around us know how to serve us and can offer us referrals, information, and access to prime opportunities.

How Does Personal Brand Affect Your Career Transition?

Your personal brand differentiates and distinguishes you from the masses. Studies show that employment recruiters see an average of 250 resumes for every open job they have on their desk. The typical recruiter might have seven to ten positions they are trying to fill. That's an average of 1,750 to 2,500 resumes floating past that recruiter's desk. How could they possibly read, evaluate, assess, and understand each one with that workload?

Recruiters note that when a resume jumps out at them—relates to the position they are hiring for, clarifies how the candidate fits the requirements, and showcases the applicant's personal brand—it gets noticed above others.

Your personal brand also empowers and entices others to advocate and endorse you. When people feel they know you and what you stand for, they are more comfortable supporting and helping you. Similarly, when your network feels they know what you can offer and what you are looking for, they are more likely to refer you to opportunities and let you use their name to gain access to prime positions. Transfer of credibility—what happens when someone allows you to use their name or relationship with you to advance yourself—requires a great deal of trust and must be founded on a solid personal brand. For instance, I get several emails each week from veterans who seek to access my network or request that I forward their resume to my contacts. These veterans know that I have great professional relationships with influencers in many desirable markets. But when someone who heard me speak at a conference, or read an article I wrote, or met me three years ago asks me to forward their information to someone I value in my network, they've asked me to vouch for them. Without realizing it, this person has asked me to put my name and credibility on the line to promote them. If I know the veteran and am comfortable doing so, that's fine. But where there is little existing relationship, where I'm not sure about this person's track record or credentials, and where I risk looking foolish to my valued network, I'm less likely to comply.

How Is Personal Brand Different from Reputation?

Personal brand is a result of you intentionally shaping how you want to be seen, judged, and perceived. It should be the intention, behavior, and communication you set out to others, although if you don't direct your personal brand, others will form one for you. As I often say, "Everyone has a personal brand, by design or by default."

Your reputation, in contrast, is how others see you and what they believe to be true about you. Reputation is how you are perceived, and perception is real to the person experiencing it. Personal branding strategy gives you the ability to direct your reputation in more thoughtful, strategic, and purposeful ways. Without a strong personal brand, your reputation can be misleading, ambiguous, or even negative.

You have a great deal of control over your personal brand and, therefore, your reputation. There are other factors that impact reputation, such as environmental factors, stereotypes, emotional filters others use to judge, and so on. The best chance you have for a reputation that is meaningful, authentic, and consistent with your goals and values is to drive a strong personal brand into the market. Doing this gives others the opportunity to perceive you in the way you want.

Steps to Building Your Personal Brand

Building your personal brand is actually quite simple. It's not nearly as complicated as what you were trained for in the military. That said, it's not easy. Over the course of this chapter, I'll ask you to consider questions and ideas that will push you out of your comfort zone. The reason I do this is because you must develop a greater self-awareness and become an expert on yourself before someone else can consider you.

When you uncover your unique and interesting assets, design a personal brand strategy using your values as a guide, and then deploy your plan to build a post-military career, you put yourself in a position in which you have power and control over your future.

Step 1: Discover

The first step in personal branding is to discover who you are. Start by asking yourself some tough questions—questions you likely haven't considered before. What are your core values? What are you passionate about? What skills did you develop in the military and what are you naturally good at? What kinds of people do you most enjoy working with? At the end of your life, what is the legacy you want to leave behind?

I will walk you through the process of answering these questions for yourself and then show you how to bring it all together to formulate your personal branding statement. First, let's inventory what you believe in and stand for (your values).

What Are Your Core Values?

Every individual operates from a set of values and guiding principles, which they use to make all decisions. Perhaps your values led you to military service and kept you grounded and focused on your commitment while you wore the uniform. During your time in the military, you found many like-minded individuals who also committed to the greater values of the United States Armed Forces and the specific values of your branch and nature of service. Over time, your values expectedly became shaped by military values, including integrity, honor, service, duty, and so on.

Now I'm asking you to reflect on your values as a human being. What do you stand for? What are your nonnegotiables, and how do you define them at a granular level?

This question may have you stumped. Perhaps you have never considered this before (I hear this a lot), or you are challenged with differentiating military values (such as integrity, honor, duty, service) from your personal values (which may be similar to those military values, or not). This is normal.

Close your eyes and consider your life's story to this point: What have you stood for and fought for with passion and conviction? What guides have you used to get you to this place? What filters have you evaluated all critical decisions through? Which moral codes do you operate from?

Your values will feel deeply personal. They are yours! Before others can understand *what* you value and *how* you can share your gifts, you need to be clear on what you stand for and *why* you are passionate about these things.

Define your values in as much detail as possible. Resist the urge to simply list what you think I want to read or what you've been told are good values to promote. Your values must be so specific and clear to you that they are nonnegotiable and unquestionable when you consider their ability to direct your life.

Consider this example: I led a workshop with a team of transitioning Air Force officers, and we were discussing values. One airman mentioned that his values revolved around honesty. He felt this was the root of his value set. I asked him to define "honesty" for the group. He explained that honesty to him meant an unequivocal commitment to always telling the truth, no matter what, 100 percent, no questions asked. Following up, I asked if he had children, to which he proudly proclaimed, "Yes! A 12- and 14-year-old!" To clarify, I asked how he'd explained the whole Santa Claus fantasy when his kids were younger. Had he been honest about Santa's existence with his children? As the color drained from his face and he stammered, I explained that my point wasn't to catch him in a lie but to help him clarify "honesty."

I then presented him with a scenario to consider: "What if," I asked, "we left the building and outside there were television crews with cameras and microphones. If one of those reporters asked you to clarify a news story unfolding within your team inside the building, how honest would you be (and you were not able to defer to your public affairs officer)?

I presented this scenario because I knew there are limits imposed by him by the military on sharing confidential information. If he were to be completely honest—his expressed value—and answered the reporter, he'd likely be fired and arrested for sharing confidential information.

Realizing this, the officer had to reassess his value of complete honesty. Together, we concluded that more specific words to communicate honesty, such as "candor," and "appropriate truthfulness," were a clearer basis for his value set.

The point here is that your value definition is not something to be taken lightly. You need to think carefully about what you value and then find words that reflect the depth and breadth of your belief around those values. These values are the foundation of your brand and the basis for the career choices you'll make.

Actions that support your values and confirm that you "walk the talk" are important to demonstrate credibility for the values. Without proof that you are committed to living your life in alignment with the values, your "values" mean little. Values without action are not credible.

Action

Identify four to five values that you believe define you and that you could comfortably defend. Get as detailed into those values as you possibly can. Then assign examples of actions you've taken throughout your career to live and uphold those values. Write them down in this way:

- Value:
- Action (proof):

Inventory Your Passions

- **Who inspires you?** What people in your life motivate you and push you to be better? Are there authors, speakers, thought leaders, or business leaders who inspire you and whom you follow closely?

> **Action**
>
> List the people who inspire you and why—what do you look up to them for? Why are you motivated to listen to them?

- **What excites you?** What topics, issues, causes, or subjects could you talk about endlessly and effortlessly? Maybe you could spend hours reading and discussing the use of technology to improve space travel, or you enjoy reading books about entrepreneurship and innovation, or you watch endless tutorials and videos about leadership and professional development.

> **Action**
>
> Make a list of topics that excite you.

- **What are you naturally gifted at doing?** Are you musically inclined? A good writer? Excellent with math, formulas, and patterns? What types of activities feel easy when you're doing them, as if you don't have to think to complete them?

> **Action**
>
> List what you are naturally gifted at completing.

Inventory Your Skills, Traits, and Experiences (Inside the Military and Out)

- **Which skills did you intentionally develop and hone during your time in the military?** Don't list everything you know how to do or were trained for. Instead, list the skills and talents you purposefully worked toward improving and developing during your military career. For example, if you worked as a cybersecurity expert doing intel work, you might have spent significant time learning foreign languages, understanding cultural nuances, and building relationships with people from other countries. Although your actual job would have entailed significantly more than this, if your interests were geared more to building these skills, focus there. Resist the urge to list every ability you might possibly possess.

> ### Action
>
> Make a list of your skills.

- **Which character traits most accurately and authentically describe you?** You might think of qualities such as:

Perseverant	Dedicated	Loyal	Committed
Values driven	Resilient	Brave	Candid
Hard working	Service oriented	Problem solver	
Leader	Obedient	Learner	Trainable
Calm under pressure	Quick thinker	Respectful	Team oriented

> ### Action
>
> Which of those words feel like you? Are there others? List those too.

- **Looking over your military career, what experiences highlight your value?** Here you'll focus on the experiences that are memorable to you because they highlight your expertise, passion, and skills. For example, if an experience that stands out for you was a strategy you deployed in the execution of a combat mission, consider what personal qualities you brought to the situation. Rather than list the steps you took to complete your task, focus on how you gathered intel, assessed the data, processed information, and executed the strategy to successful completion. Your training, combined with your thinking, is where the experience becomes valuable going forward.

> **Action**
>
> List the experiences you've had that showcase your expertise, passion, and skills. What did you do (specifically) that made those experiences valuable to your career?

Consider the Types of People You Work Well With

- **What types of people do you enjoy working with (from a style perspective)?** These are the people you've been tasked to work with where it feels effortless and enjoyable. Perhaps you enjoy working with people who are analytical and process information after thoughtful consideration. Or maybe you prefer more spontaneous and impulsive people who are willing to take risks with less data and input. Do you enjoy people with large personalities, who fill the room when they laugh or tell a story? Are you more comfortable around people who work independently and quietly?

> **Action**
>
> List the traits and attributes of the people you enjoy working with the most (from a style perspective).

- **What types of people do you enjoy working with (from a values perspective)?** Thinking outside of the military now, what values need to be present for you to work well with someone? Do they need to share your commitment to service or a dedicated work ethic? Could you work alongside or for someone who lacked integrity? How would you define integrity?

> **Action**
>
> List the values you need to be present for you to work successfully with someone.

List Some Ways You'd Like Ultimately to Be Remembered

We call this your "desired reputation," and it comes to life in your legacy, the ideal end state of reputation you set for yourself based on your life. When you imagine the impact you'll have on others and the way you'd like them to remember you, what words come to mind?

Since brands are anchored in feelings, think about how you'd like people around you to feel about who you are and why you're here. As you move through your career, the way others regard you often has more to do with how they feel about you than with what they know about your skills or technical acumen. You may apply for a position where you don't have enough experience. The hiring manager could feel that you are worth taking a chance on and offer you the opportunity. Or you may ask someone in your network to refer you to a potential client, and they're willing to do so because they feel you can be trusted and will represent them well. Feelings drive actions.

Action

What words describe the reputation you want for yourself? Focus on the feelings words more than the analytical words. Consider beginning with

I want people around me to feel I am _____ and that I'll deliver _____. Then they will feel _____ toward me.

Tie It All Together

Now gather the lists you've made and create a series of statements that reflect who you are, your strengths, and the kinds of people you'd like to work with. This list of statements is your "asset inventory," which we will use to create your personal branding strategy in Step 2.

Asset Inventory

My values anchor in:

I'm passionate about:

I'm skilled at:

I stand out for my abilities to:

I'm natural at:

I prefer to work with people who are:

I want to be remembered as:

Step 2: Design a Personal Branding Action Plan for Your Career

With your asset inventory in hand (Step 1) and your career goals, discussed in earlier chapters, now you'll create a plan to get there. The process of formulating your personal brand and turning it into an action plan is not linear and formulaic. As you grow in your career, you'll add to your assets, goals, and experiences. As a result, your asset inventory will grow, and your action plan will change.

There are four parts to your personal brand action plan:

1 Assess your asset inventory and offers.

2 Clarify the needs and wants of your intended audience.

3 Identify self-marketing tools to deploy to build your reputation.

4 Add tools for assessment, evaluation, and course correction as you build your personal brand over time.

Assess Your Asset Inventory and Offers

In the previous section, you listed various assets you will bring into your next career. We looked at your passions, values, skills, the kinds of people you enjoy working with, and how you ultimately want to be remembered. Now let's see what patterns emerge.

Do you see any themes from what you listed?

- **Are you drawn to certain types of projects and people?** For instance, do creative endeavors excite you more than analytical ones? When you've had most of your success, has it been because you were in the lead role or did you focus more on implementation?

- **Do your actions consistently support your values?** Or have there been instances where your work required you to act in conflict with your values? If so, how did you manage that? Why did you feel compelled to repeat this behavior?

- **Based on what you did before, do you feel motivated to do the same or different work in your next career?** This question might be obvious if your job in the military is not transferrable to the private sector. (If you were a sniper in the Marine Corps, for example, there isn't a high demand for snipers in the civilian sector.) If you were a logistician in the Army, are you considering logistics, supply chain, or even project management in your post-military career?

Clarify the Needs and Wants of Your Intended Audience

Your personal brand will need to be relevant and compelling to an intended audience who is attracted to people like you, with experiences and skills you offer, and who can add value in the ways you can. Those are the people who will become your employers, network contacts, advocates, and referral sources.

Think back to the list you made of the types of people you get along with, whom you enjoy working with. Can you imagine the kinds of jobs or type of work they do? Are they in positions of leadership or influence? If you can, identify people who might fit into your target audience.

Now consider what those people care about—what do they need to know about you in order to want to have a conversation or possibly work with you? Do they need to know you have training that is relevant to what they hire for? Do they need to know you have advanced certifications? Do they need to know you prefer to work independently?

Next, what do those people need to feel about you? Answering this is harder. Consider what they care about and how that transfers to you. If they care about team building and collaboration, they might need to feel that you are able to work well with others. They might need to feel you bring leaderships skills and are willing to mentor those around you. Perhaps they need to feel you are easy to work with and would fit into their company culture.

Later, when we discuss positioning yourself for the application and interview process, you will see how this thinking will serve you well. If you can speak the language of your intended audience, highlighting what they need to know and feel, you are in a better position to establish rapport, build trust, and form relationships that emphasize mutual benefit.

Identify Self-Marketing Tools to Deploy to Build Your Reputation

Building your post-military reputation will require you to position yourself consistently and confidently across many channels and tools. Although resumes and cover letters will certainly play a part in your self-marketing, so will your online profiles, networking strategies and contacts, personal narrative, and body language and presence (image). Think about these self-marketing tools as an integrated ecosystem of your professional posture: How you show up on paper (your resume) should coordinate with your LinkedIn profile, support how you speak about yourself, and dovetail into the language your network uses to introduce or refer you. Self-marketing works when it's consistent and credible, not when it's a stand-alone effort.

Consider these questions as you think about the way you currently market yourself:

- Do you have an updated modular resume that highlights your experiences and value?
- Have you refined your elevator pitch—the way you introduce yourself to others?
- Are your online reputation assets (i.e., LinkedIn profile) updated and consistent with your goals?
- Have you started building a network of contacts who will support, guide, mentor, and refer you?
- Have you received feedback on your body language, either positive or negative?

- Are you prepared to dress for interviews and your next job? Or is your wardrobe still military uniforms?

There will be many opportunities throughout this book to refine and assess your self-marketing assets and goals. For now, think about where you might be strongest and where your weaknesses lie.

Add Tools for Assessment, Evaluation, and Course Correction as You Build Your Personal Brand over Time

As you progress through your career, you will undoubtedly experience success and setbacks, opportunities and challenges. Throughout all of it, your personal brand action plan should adapt to your new environment.

Feedback and assessments—whether formal or informal—will offer insight about your reputational growth and the health of your personal brand. These check-ins allow you to confirm that what you're doing is working for you (to your advantage) and will help you identify those behaviors that are irrelevant or working against you.

Examples of tools to assess your reputation might include:

- **Career assessments.** Is your career reinforcing your development in ways that expand your reach and influence over those you want to serve? Career assessment tools can shed light on areas you still need to refine and develop as well as reassure you of your progress.

- **Insight from your network.** The professional relationships you will strategically develop should serve you (and permit you to serve them too). If you find that you are investing more time in serving others than you see in return, this could indicate that you need to adjust the types of people you are targeting for networking or the quality of those engagements. Similarly, if your network consistently refers you to ideal opportunities, that is confirmation that your contacts know what you offer, can identify opportunities for you, and are confident and comfortable referring you.

- **Feedback at work.** Over time, you will likely receive feedback and evaluations from your team and supervisors. Read these through a few lenses. Consider:

- How sufficiently are you completing your job?
- Are there areas for improvement in the quality of work you deliver?
- Are there indications you are valued for your work and your contributions?
- Are you delivering just what's expected of you and not standing out?

Look for patterns in the feedback and evaluations you receive that either confirm you are presenting yourself authentically and aligned with your strategy or not. If not, course correction is warranted.

- **Surveying and polling your contacts.** In my work as a personal branding coach, we often survey client contacts to assess perception. We ask questions to gauge how the client is regarded, what they are best known for, and what value they offer. Periodically my clients revisit that feedback and sometimes readminister the surveys to see if their key contacts have noticed any changes. Seeing positive shifts in your contacts' perception of and attitude toward you is a good indicator you are moving in the right direction.

- **Check in with yourself.** From time to time, ask yourself if you feel fulfilled in your work, if the people you spend your days with appreciate and understand you, and if you feel you are moving in the direction of your desired reputation and legacy. When things are off, we typically feel it. Give yourself permission to check in with yourself and listen to what doesn't feel right. Similarly, when you feel confirmation that your choices are working out and your career path supports your values and goals, you'll have the personal encouragement to continue forward.

Step 3: Deploy Your Strategy to Ensure Consistent and Confident Communication of Your Values, Goals, and Mission

After taking the time to discover your personal assets, interests, and values, to evaluate your target audience and opportunities, and then to design a personal brand action plan to build your career path, it's time to deploy your brand and build your reputation.

Over your career life cycle, deploying your strategy requires similar steps to your work in the military: You'll **clarify** your objectives and create personal brand goals (mission), **distill** them down to manageable steps and formulate a personal brand action plan, and then **apply** what you decide in actions.

Clarifying objectives means you consider how you are perceived today, how you want to be perceived, and how wide/narrow the gap between them is. Filling in the gap between how you are known today and how you want to be known becomes the goal of your personal branding efforts. For example, if you are currently perceived as stubborn, hard to get along with, and abrupt yet you'd like to be seen as someone who can bring bold ideas into static teams, who will confidently take the lead when others hide, and who will always have her team's back, then you have some work to do. You may need to consciously change the way you communicate or behave around your team. This is not about changing who you are (and what you feel, need, and want), but your strategy and plan may warrant that you modify your behavior to achieve your desired reputation. You'll need to determine which steps and actions you should take to show your intended audience that your perceived weaknesses (i.e., stubbornness, abruptness) can be pivoted into strengths (willingness to lead in adverse conditions).

Then, distilling down the objectives into manageable steps and a clear personal brand action plan requires you to consider all aspects of your transition and all of the tools we discussed earlier (social media, body language, narrative, network, etc.). Using this same example, to shift being seen as arrogant or noncollaborative, you might share more personal stories of challenge and success, ask better questions of your network to show you care about their career progress and not just your own, or publicly praise teammates when they do something worth celebrating.

The final step is living this brand. Every day, every action, every relationship should reflect your commitment to living your brand and values. When your intended audience sees you living consistently with what you profess to stand for and represent, over time they will trust your brand.

The veteran who is considered too hard to work with can, over time, show that she's driven and passionate, not difficult. The veteran who wants to be seen as a servant leader can seek personal and professional opportunities to help those less fortunate and to mentor those stuck in their career path, and can offer inspiration to those he's never met via social media.

Measuring Results

As you deploy your personal brand strategy, it will be important to measure and monitor results. Measuring and monitoring the impact of your brand is more than looking at your resume and ensuring that each job outperforms the last one. You'll be looking for signs of consistency, integration of your values, and increases in meaning and contribution for each position you hold.

For example, I articulate my two core values—gratitude and generosity—into the marketing of my business, and my work. As I mentioned, the title of my TEDx Talk is *The Power of Gratitude and Generosity: Serving Those Who've Served.* I measure and monitor my success in communicating my brand values by the feedback I get after I deliver a speech or when someone connects with me on LinkedIn or emails me after reading one of my books. When they refer to me as "generous" or recognize that my actions stem from my sense of gratitude, I know my personal brand strategy is working.

In order for your values to resonate with others as authentic, they must be rooted in your true feelings and beliefs about how you'll live your life. This is how others can learn to trust and rely on you.

An additional measure of the success of your personal brand strategy includes looking at the opportunities you attract. If your goal is to be positioned as a caring and driven leader, for instance, and you are increasingly given opportunities to lead projects and teams, that's a good sign that your efforts to build a credible brand are working.

By contrast, if you find yourself passed up for promotions or job opportunities that include a leadership path, you might not be representing yourself correctly or consistently, which requires going back to Step 1: Discover and reassessing your data. Did you evaluate your current reputation correctly? Is your target audience aligned with your desired positioning? Did you adequately articulate (to yourself initially) what a "caring and driven leader" looks like and how they act?

Then you should want to evaluate your strategy under Step 2: Design. Did you skip steps, believing you didn't need to complete them? Were you overly confident in your actions, sending the message that your leadership aspirations were premature? Did you fail to consider the needs and feelings of the people you wanted to lead, thereby alienating them as you sought control?

Run back through the process when things go well to identify where your insight and information worked best. Replicate what works!

As you move through your post-military career, and particularly when things aren't progressing as you'd hoped, refer to the personal branding process to find the blind spots or gaps you may have missed. Allow yourself to look at your progress through the three-step process—Discover (self-assessment and understanding of target audience), Design a Personal Branding Action Plan for Your Career (goal setting and strategy development), and Deploy Your Strategy to Ensure Consistent and Confident Communication of Your Values, Goals, and Mission (applying your personal brand)—with an open mind and heart. This is your career and it's important that you see things clearly, from all angles.

Your Personal Brand Is Your Legacy

Focus on presenting yourself with clarity and confidence. Your personal brand is how you want to show up in the world. It's how you'll position yourself to ensure you're viewed as compelling and relevant to your intended audience.

A strong personal brand does not ensure that your reputation is flawless—mistakes happen, environments shift, reputation crisis can occur outside of our control. But, with a focused personal brand strategy, you ensure there is more context around who you are and what you stand for beyond just your resume.

As we've seen here, your personal brand requires deep discovery and insight, a well-designed plan and strategy to bring your personal and professional assets forward, and the diligence and patience to deploy your gifts into the marketplace where they are rewarded and appreciated.

In Closing

Your personal brand is the asset you'll use to position your strengths, goals, desires, talents, and the value you can offer to others in your target audience. When you drive your personal brand and are strategic about the opportunities you pursue in building your brand (as well as the ones you turn down because they don't align with your desired brand), you will attract people who want what you can offer. It's when we are unclear, unfocused, and unsure of who we are and what we can share that we attract random, disconnected, and unfulfilling arrangements.

The steps to create and manage your personal brand to build a positive reputation might feel cumbersome and uncomfortable. This is normal. In the many years I've coached and trained military service members and veterans on the concept of personal branding and reputation management, I've seen the contorted and confused faces of my audiences... until they get used to the idea that they are being asked to learn about themselves in order to promote themselves to others.

Spend the time to uncover your personal and professional assets, clarify who you'd like to work with (target audience), and thoughtfully use the tools available (through your narrative, social media, network, image, and body language) to bring the best version of yourself forward to attract the opportunities you desire.

Career-Ready Tools to Gather

05

Resume and Cover Letter

When you started your military career, you were trained on what you'd need to know, ran drills to be prepared, and were handed the tools you'd need to be successful. From a uniform to written standards to equipment to arms, you had what you needed to do your job and complete the mission as required.

Think of preparing for your new career in the same way, except that now you will have to search out and gather all the tools, resources, and assets you'll need to succeed. Although you will be provided with many books, articles, videos, mentors, coaches, and advisors, you will be responsible for using them to serve your new career in the way you deem most appropriate.

The tools you'll gather now are specific and targeted to get you from where you are now (the starting point) to where you want to go (a successful career). These tools are modular, evolving, and suitable to your current situation and future goals. For instance, if you are pursuing education after the military, your resume (one tool) will be more focused on finding short-term internships, part-time work, and apprenticeships rather than attracting a permanent, long-term employer. If you are pursuing employment, you'll need tools focused on identifying ideal employers, gathering the career assets that will make you marketable to them, and positioning strategies to place you in the best light with those companies.

Your resume, cover letter, LinkedIn profile, and other social media accounts are all means of communicating your value to recruiters, networking contacts, peers, and interviewers. Ensure that the message you are communicating about yourself is consistent across all of these outlets. Consistency and continuity mean that what is read on paper about you is validated by what your networking contact (who walked your resume into the recruiter's office) says about you and is reinforced by what they find online about you. Think holistically and strategically to ensure your career tools are working in your favor.

Since each of these tools will take time, effort, and some resources to develop, decide how quickly you need to have each piece ready.

Begin gathering and refining assets you'll need, such as your resume, cover letters, digital profiles, personal narrative, networking contacts and networking strategy, and mentors.

Next identify the resources or tools for which you'll need some outside help. You may want to hire a resume writer to create or refine your resume or work with a career coach to refine your interpersonal communication skills to help you with networking. It will take time to find and engage the right people to help you. Budget the costs and create a timeline to effectively integrate their work into your overall career transition.

Finally, identify any gaps that exist for you right now. Are your goals greater than your abilities? Are your expectations realistic? Do you have access to the resources you'll need to succeed? For instance, if you want to be a business owner but don't have much business experience, you will need to allocate time to work for a business that will teach you the skills to be successful or pursue a master's degree in business.

The Resume

Resumes matter. Recruiters and hiring managers use them to assess whether a candidate has the requisite skills and experience to fill the role they have available.

Large companies use computer algorithms that search resumes for specific keywords that are relevant to that role, company, and industry. Recruiters and hiring professionals are inundated with resumes for every open position they advertise, so it is important to make sure that your resume includes the right keywords for the position, company, and industry. On average, human readers of resumes (recruiters, hiring managers, and resume screeners) spend six seconds scanning and reviewing resumes for relevant keywords, experiences, and skills. Whether your resume is scanned by a human or a computer, if it doesn't map to the skills they need for the job, you risk being passed over.

How to Get Started Writing a Resume

There are few things as intimidating as writing your first resume. Whether you are a college student or retiring Marine, the blank page of your first resume can fill you with dread. Instead of worrying about formatting or choosing the font size or layout, begin by listing information as you think of it.

Start by capturing and outlining information into these areas.

Header/Contact Information

It might be tempting to list every way possible to reach you, but be practical. Often employers prefer to contact candidates by email, but recruiters and hiring managers recognize that younger workers prefer texting as a primary means of contact. Be sure your mobile phone number is on your resume.

- **Name.** At the top of the document, put your name. If you plan to use a nickname you're commonly known by, put it in parentheses between your first and last name.

- **Mailing address.** You don't have to list your home address. In fact, some resume experts advise against it for security reasons. If you plan to relocate after separation, aren't in permanent housing (i.e., perhaps living with your family), or desire privacy, it is fine to omit your residential address.

- **Phone number.** List a cell or mobile phone number, not a home or landline. Children can answer the home phone and that might send the wrong impression, particularly if the child is in the middle of a temper tantrum. Also, you'll likely have your cell phone with you when you're not at home, making it easy to reach you. Ensure your voicemail is professional and succinct. No need for a lengthy message or explanation of why you can't answer the phone. Just state your name (this really helps with pronunciation if your name is tricky, like mine!) and that you'll return the call as soon as possible. If you feel inclined, you can also offer your email address as an alternative way to reach you if the message is important.

- **Email.** Your resume is a document of professional nature, and your email address should also reflect professionalism. The goal of your email address should be to make you reachable. Sometimes service members create fun or playful email addresses while in the service. For a resume and job search, your email should be more professional. Consider using your first and last name and then your email host. For instance, you could use JohnSmith@. If that name is already taken, add a middle initial or other identifier, like JohnTSmith@ or John.T.Smith2019@. The type of service you use (Gmail, Hotmail, Yahoo, etc.) is less important than the name. Employers don't enjoy having to type BigDaddy@gmail.com into their computer. If you will be using your name, consider capitalizing the first letters of each word to make it more readable, such as JohnASmith@gmail.com.

- **Online profiles.** Many job seekers also include the URL of their LinkedIn profiles or personal websites. These are completely appropriate on a resume, as they indicate where readers can find more information about you.

Experience Section

- What jobs have you done? By position, list the titles and responsibilities you had in each role, including those you had prior to military service. If you can demilitarize your experience into a civilian equivalent, great. If not, we'll get to that shortly. Just get everything on paper at this point.

- Under each job you've held, list accomplishments, successes, and results achieved. If you question whether a job is significant or not, list them all for now. You can edit them out later.

- List the number of people you managed and the dollar value of programs or equipment you were responsible for.

- Catalog any training or certification you received for each job.

- Quantify all results, if possible. Recruiters want to see tangible proof that you're a "leader, problem solver" and someone who's "passionate about business." Just stating those things doesn't get a reader's attention; they want to see results listed as numbers, data, and supporting information.

- Write down anything significant, interesting, or impactful that happened to which you had to react or respond while you held that position.

Skills and Credentials

- What skills, training, certifications, and credentials did you receive or earn while in uniform? Even if you took classes outside of your "day job" or pursued training while on terminal leave, list it. You can always delete it later if it's not relevant or necessary.

Internships, Apprenticeships, and Fellowships

- List any internships, apprenticeships, and fellowships you may have had prior to separation. Be specific about where you worked, what you did, and what you learned. If possible, quantify your results.

Volunteer Work

- List and describe any volunteer work you've done. If relevant, specify why you chose that type of work or constituency to serve. Also list the responsibilities you held, the impact of your volunteerism, and any achievements or recognition you received.

Education

- What education do you have? Have you completed any college credits? Do you have a master's degree? It is recommended that you list your education this way: the name of your school, location, degree obtained, graduation year. Include your GPA if it's above 3.4. Also list add any significant honors or academic recognition, relevant coursework, leadership positions held, extracurricular activities, or other achievements.

Also inventory what parts of your past experiences you enjoyed the most. This is not a section on the resume, but it will be important as you refine your resume into a modular document. List the individual aspects of each job that made you happy, that you felt were most fulfilling, and that you felt best doing.

If this is your first resume, a chronological format will likely work best. Be sure to include the dates and locations of each position you list.

For more advanced resumes, use whatever format is accepted as standard for your industry—chronological, functional, combination, biographical, or curriculum vitae (CV).

The Modular Resume Is King

No matter what resume format you choose, you should be able to tailor it to the specific position or experience for which you are applying. A resume is not a one-size-fits-all, generic document that is sent to any employer for any job. Think of your resume as a modular, flexible tool.

In addition to relevant skills and appropriate experience, each employer will want to see examples of career successes that indicate culture fit, ability to perform in the particular company's business climate, a passion for the industry/business/work, and other qualities in an ideal candidate.

To increase your chances of consideration, update and tweak your resume to highlight related experience, skills, expertise, and talents and use language that is specific to that industry or company. Consider designing your resume in a flexible and modular format, so you can easily update, change, and refine sections to suit the needs, keywords, and tone of the job for which you're applying. A modular resume enables you to customize your resume to the company's values, vision, mission, and use their language to get the attention of the recruiter who is evaluating your fit for the job. Depending on the job requirements, you may leave sections of your resume out (e.g., you might omit your hobbies and interests if the company wouldn't value them) and include others (you might replace your lists of job experiences with lists of skill keywords if the job application emphasizes this requirement.)

Should You Hire a Resume Writer?

Finding a civilian job is challenging enough if you are a good or adequate writer. If putting your words into an organized resume seems too daunting, it may make sense to enlist help.

There are numerous independent sources for resume assistance—from consultants to online templates to friends. Many nonprofit organizations also offer resume counsel at no or reduced cost.

In hiring a writer to craft your post-military resume, consider these tips:

- **Choose someone who is familiar with the career you're coming from (the military) and the types of jobs you'll be applying for.**

- **Don't just "demilitarize" your skills on your resume.** The skills and experience listed on your resume should relate directly to the target employer you want to attract.

- **Take an active role in the crafting of your resume.** Be sure you are involved in how your experience is described, the value you provided, and what your past says about who you are. Too often, veterans simply accept what a professional writer crafts for them and then can't answer questions or speak to their resume in a job interview.

- **Get comfortable speaking about your successes.** A benefit of hiring a resume writer is that they will help draw out your accomplishments and results from you. Although you might be reluctant to brag, they won't be.

Make Sure Your Resume Pops

Once you've crafted the content of your resume, consider how interesting or eye-catching the resume should be. Design can be distracting, but an overly dense and unformatted resume can be hard to read. Strive for clean, professional, and attractive, minimizing distractions (crazy fonts, emoticons, icons, stock images, etc.) and making sure your most important information is easy to find. Keep the margins wide and the font readable. If you're trying to squeeze in too much information, you make your resume harder for recruiters to read.

When you apply for jobs, you'll likely send your resume to an employer in a PDF format or enter sections of your resume into an online application tool. For this reason, always keep your resume in its original state (e.g., as a Word or Pages document) and save it as a PDF under the same name.

What Can You Safely Leave Out of Your Resume?

When deciding how much to include in your resume, you'll likely fall into one of two camps: Either you'll be hesitant to list your career accomplishments or you'll overdo it. Employers see many resumes that read like life stories rather than career summaries.

If you're tempted to include everything you've ever done, remember this: Employers have a short attention span in reviewing resumes. I worked with an Army Master Sergeant named John on his resume, and he struggled with leaving off what he thought was critical content. His career had, admittedly, been rich with challenges and successes. He felt he was doing a disservice to his past if he left anything off his resume. His resume was six pages, single spaced.

We worked together to research the employers he was targeting. They liked directness; they appreciated candor, focus, and results. I convinced John that if he continued to pursue this employer with a six-page resume, he was communicating that he lacked focus and directness. The onus was on him to be intentional, specific, and focused in how he communicated his value. Was this hard for him? Definitely! But the employer appreciated John's ability to target his skills and experiences as they aligned with the company goals and saw how he might fit in with their bold initiatives.

When Should You Update or Modify Your Resume?

If you create a modular resume, you'll save different versions of your resume in an easy-to-find naming system. For instance, you might have resumes that are titled by date:

John.Smith.Resume.November2019

John.Smith.January2020

Or you could name them more specifically by area of focus:

JohnSmith.Resume.ProjectMgmt

JohnSmith.Resume.OrganizationalDev

JohnSmith.Resume.Operations

As you gain more experience, skills, credentials, or insight about the job you are applying for, you'll update your resume. I suggest you keep each version of your resume (sort them by date in your filing system so you know which is most recent) as you may eliminate content and replace it with new information. Over time, you may wish to refer to something you removed from your resume a year ago. If you sort them by date (and don't simply overwrite your one resume), you'll be able to find the previous sections.

Think of your resume as a living document—it should be updated and modified as needed. Just as one resume won't work for every job opening, neither will last year's resume reflect who you are today, a year later.

Resumes Should Focus on Keywords

Employers today use keywords to sort skills, experience, credentials, and certifications. Without keyword searches, someone reading a resume might be challenged to determine qualifications of the candidate.

Keywords are search words or terms. And what matters the most is the keywords the employer uses to search, not the ones you believe best reflect your skills. If you use the wrong keyword, the employer won't notice you. Simple as that.

Employers highlight keywords they care about on their websites (especially in describing company culture and work environment), in job descriptions, on their LinkedIn profiles, and anywhere else they describe the company and who they hire. It's critical to learn the keywords that matter to your target company and then sprinkle them (where appropriate and truthful) into your resume.

Here's an example of how this works: Near the top of his resume, John used to say "Transitioning Air Force officer, cyber intel background, seeking position in Boston."

After speaking with John, I learned he really wanted to work in a fast-growing company that had a fun "work hard and play hard" culture and where he'd work alongside international colleagues. He identified three companies that met his criteria and that sponsored cybersecurity products and systems for clients to ensure they could protect themselves and their families. These companies promoted business values of collaboration, innovation, and protection. These were the companies John wanted to attract, but his resume didn't speak their language.

John and I reworked his materials: He wove the words "passionate, committed, and guardian" into his LinkedIn profile when describing why his work in the military was so meaningful. He also brought those sentiments and keywords over to his resume and rewrote his opening as:

> After 15 years in the Air Force, where I served to protect and defend systems and people I care deeply for, I'm committed to growing my career in cybersecurity in the Boston area. Today, I am looking to align with a growing company that is as passionate as I am to values of innovation and collaboration and protecting those we serve.

After these changes, his resume got noticed.

In other examples, become mindful of keywords that don't exactly translate your military job or work into civilian language but are close. For instance, you may have been in personnel management, but civilian employers call that human resources. You may have been a medic in the Army but civilian employers highlight keywords of healthcare professional or medical personnel.

Keywords will be entered into resumes, cover letters, online applications, and even conversations. Make sure you're consistently using the keywords your target employer uses and is searching for.

Resume Mistakes to Avoid

Before you start sending out your resume to potential employers, ensure you haven't made any of the next common mistakes.

- **Unfocused.** An unfocused resume forces the reader to figure out who the applicant is and what the applicant is able to offer. Your resume looks unfocused if you simply list what you've done without helping the reader see the story: What have you done in your career that led you here? What steps and decisions did you make with each promotion or job that set you up for success today and tomorrow? How did you perform on each job based on what you had to work with? Employers want to see you focused on the kind of work they're hiring for.

- **Missing metrics and results.** Similar to the last mistake, if the descriptions of your previous work leave out the results or impact of that work, you're missing an important element. Employers want to see what you accomplished and the benefits of those outcomes to your employer (in this case, the military).

- **Grammar and spelling mistakes.** If you have several people (friends, mentors, family) review your resume in advance, they will (hopefully) catch spelling or grammatical errors. It's not enough to rely on your computer's spellcheck software, since many words are correctly spelled, just incorrectly used. Employers may disregard a resume with errors on it. Errors could indicate inattention to detail, sloppiness, or simple disregard for the importance of the document. Either way, ensure your resume is free from any errors.

- **Too heavily military.** If you haven't made your previous work experience understandable for employers, they may look past your potential. Civilianizing your resume means ensuring someone can understand what you did and the impact you created (result) whether they served in the military or not. Remember, not every branch of service speaks the same way, so even if the person reading your resume is a veteran, their understanding could be way off from yours if they served in a different branch of the military.

- **Inaccurate or misleading information.** You should never, ever lie or mislead on your resume. Overinflating your skills or experiences, lying about where you were or what you achieved, or posting inaccurate degrees or certifications is typically an immediate disqualification. If a recruiter strongly suspects, or verifies, that you lied on your resume, you could be flagged from being considered for any position at the company, not just the job for which you applied.

- **Irrelevant, personal information.** There are many things that should never be listed on a resume unless there is a compelling reason the employer needs to know. For instance, an employer cannot legally ask you about your marital status, family composition, race, ethnicity, sexual orientation, and religion. Do not volunteer such information on your resume. Similarly, you do not have to reveal any physical or mental limitations or disabilities on a resume, unless they directly impact your ability to do the work. If this is the case and, for instance, you want to work as a stocker in a warehouse but are in a wheelchair, then consider whether this is the best position for you.

- **Inconsistencies.** If you switch formatting on the resume—for instance, from a chronological resume to a functional one—you'll confuse readers. Similarly, if you show a bulleted list of responsibilities and accomplishments under some jobs and not others, it can beg the question: "What happened at this job?"

Your goal is to show consistency across your resume. By formatting the document uniformly and ensuring that each part of the resume tells the story of your career (indicating what you can do next), your resume becomes a valuable part of your career path.

Action

Run your resume through this checklist:

☐ Research the companies and industries you'll target in advance. Ensure your resume speaks to them and shows how you'll add value if selected for an opportunity.

☐ Check the formatting of your resume. Ensure it's attractive but not distracting. Eliminate any design elements that don't support your story as a candidate.

☐ Enlist several people to proofread your resume for grammar, spelling, and continuity of message and format.

☐ Check for military speak. Whenever possible, speak in the language of your target employer.

☐ Use the keywords the employer or industry uses.

☐ Ensure everything you claim on your resume is true and accurate.

☐ Put your name and contact information on each page of your resume. Include this information at the top of the title page and in the footer on subsequent pages in case the pages get separated.

The Cover Letter

I love cover letters. A cover letter is just that, a letter that provides a unique and wonderful way to tell your story to an employer. It is a brief document that typically accompanies a resume when emailed, mailed, or submitted for a job online. The cover letter is an introduction of who you are, what you have done, and how you can serve the company you're addressing.

Why You Should Send a Cover Letter with a Resume

If you just send a resume, without a cover letter, you are assuming the reader will understand everything about your background and connect your past to your future contribution.

A cover letter empowers you to explain any variances in your past (e.g., gaps in experiences, lack of certifications, or career path changes), connect your military career to your civilian pursuits, and clarify any challenges you've had in your career. Although your cover letter should not be a personal note to the reader sharing intimate details of your life, it is a way to communicate what might not be apparent, clear, or easily understood from reading your resume.

A cover letter can clarify:

- Why you decided to leave the military
- Why you're interested in working in this new industry/company
- Why you took time off after separating to pursue education
- Any gaps in work history
- How you see this new job fulfilling your passion and leveraging your talents

- How you can add value beyond what's written about your past
- Anything else that needs explaining or clarifying before the reader proceeds to look at your resume

Key Ingredients to a Standout Cover Letter

Your cover letter shouldn't repeat everything listed in your resume. Keep it focused and succinct. I don't advocate a specific number of paragraphs, but your cover letter should include an opening sentence or short paragraph, then a couple of targeted paragraphs explaining anything that needs to be elaborated on and concluding with an expression of gratitude for the reader's consideration.

Be sure your name and contact information are listed on each page of the cover letter, if it exceeds one page. The resume and cover letter could get separated after they are printed, and you want the reader to be able to match them up.

Always address the person you're sending the cover letter to in the first sentence (Dear Susan, or Dear Mr. Richards). Whenever possible, send your cover letter (and resume) in PDF format. This ensures all formatting and content will stay intact as your cover letter and resume are reviewed and circulated.

A standout cover letter also shares something that will get the reader's attention. If you're passionate about technology as a way to solve global challenges, say that. Concerned about how policies are being delivered in government? Let the reader know that's your career focus. Have you spent your entire life motivating and mentoring others? That would be great to highlight in your cover letter.

End your cover letter strong: Avoid just stopping the letter, and don't ramble on too long. A succinct and confident call to action, such as "I'll follow up next week to schedule a conversation," tells the reader that you'll be proactive about your career.

What to Avoid in the Cover Letter

Just because you can add more narrative to your cover letter, you shouldn't tell your life story. After all, you want to leave something for the interview. If your cover letter rambles on, provides too much background information, or is overly casual, you might turn away a reader who is likely looking for something more focused and succinct.

Be sure the formatting, style, tone, and language of your cover letter also matches your resume. If you present a polished and professional resume, keep the writing on the cover letter in the same format and tone. These two documents should look like they go together.

Keywords

As with your resume, wherever possible, reiterate important keywords in your cover letter. Be careful not to fall back on the terms or words you're most comfortable with in your cover letter. Consistency is very important.

Sample Cover Letter

An example of how a cover letter could read follows. It's not a script, so please make sure your letter sounds like you.

John Smith
John.Smith@gmail.com
(111) 222.3333
LinkedIn.com/in/johnsmith

Mary Jones
Human Resources Director
My Dream Employer
4444 Elm Street
Anytown, CA 11111

Dear Ms. Jones,

I am excited to present my resume for consideration as you recruit for the Commercial Accounts Manager position at My Dream Employer. My experience, career path, and skills make me a great match to meet the bold objectives of this position.

In particular, I'd highlight my work in the US Marine Corps, a position I retired from after 21 years of service. In that role, I was directly responsible for:

- Creating significant new efficiencies of systems and processes, reducing wait time for our customers by 40 percent
- Initiating a new communication process, resulting in increased response time for teams in the field
- Leading hundreds of talented individuals to strategically plan and deliver on complex problems, often with very limited information and resources

In the year since leaving the Marine Corps, I have relocated my family to the Anytown community, reconnected with loved ones, and traveled abroad. Refreshed and rejuvenated, I am ready to commit my skills, talents, and unique experiences to growing the vision at My Dream Employer.

I will contact you next week to discuss the possibility of a phone or in person interview.

Thank you,

John Smith

Action

- ☐ Create a cover letter template that can be modified for each submission. This will ensure you don't deviate from consistency with your resume.
- ☐ Be sure your contact information is clear and on every page.
- ☐ Address your cover letter to a person. Avoid "To whom it may concern" or "Dear sirs or ma'ams" whenever possible.
- ☐ Clarify or explain any gaps or challenges in your resume. Then discuss this in the cover letter.
- ☐ Keep your cover letter focused, succinct, and upbeat.
- ☐ End your cover letter with a specific follow-up.
- ☐ Sign your name in pen.
- ☐ Send the cover letter (along with your resume) as a PDF.

In Closing

Pulling together your career tools before you exit the military gives you the ability to feel organized and thoughtful about the ways you'll articulate your value to your contacts and potential employers.

Think about your career timeline and path forward. If you'll be entering school after the military, you might have some time to gather your resume and cover letter.

If you'll be pursuing self-employment or entrepreneurship, your resume will provide keen insight and connection to the investors, business partners, employees, and resources you'll need to successfully launch your company.

If the path you're on is to employment, the resume and cover letter will be important to getting the attention of ideal employers. The tone, language, and content you consistently promote in person and online will educate potential employers about who you are and what you can do; if you tie these tools together consistently, they build your personal brand and value for the remainder of your career.

Getting Yourself Out There

06

Crafting Your Narrative and Networking in Person

A famous Native American parable tells the story of a Cherokee grandfather talking to his son about prioritization in the face of fear. The grandfather explains that living within him are two wolves who fight each other. "One," he says, "is evil and fierce and is pulling me toward anger, self-pity, guilt, false pride, arrogance, and regret."

The other wolf, he tells his grandson, represents joy, love, hope, compassion, and possibility. "These two wolves fight inside me," the grandfather continues. The grandson asks which wolf will win the fight. "The one I feed," replies the grandfather.

Getting out of your comfort zone will feel scary and unnatural, but it will also bring opportunity and possibility. If you consider this as a step in the direction of your future goals, you can be more confident and positive in the face of any challenges.

In this chapter, we focus on crafting your personal narrative and elevator pitch and how you can use these tools to help you introduce yourself during in-person networking and at job fairs.

The Narrative

Your personal and professional narrative is the way you speak about yourself to yourself, the way you speak about yourself to others, and the way others speak about you. The words and phrases you use to describe yourself and your values directly impact whether and how others choose to refer, endorse, or advocate for you. Your personal narrative is a powerful career tool to develop.

Narrative—How You Speak to Yourself About Yourself

Self-talk is the way you speak to yourself. Do you affirm and reinforce your decisions and your sense of self-worth? Do you tell yourself, "I'm worthy of a happy career," or "I'm good at figuring out challenges and this transition is just a challenge…" or "I've got this!" Or do you minimize your value through negative statements, such as "I'll never get this," "I can't do this," or "No one will ever understand me"?

Positive self-talk increases confidence and reinforces your positive sense of self. Negative self-talk reduces your value and contributes to insecurity about your skills and self-worth.

In my coaching work, I frequently hear from veterans whose negative self-talk reinforces their doubts about their ability to find a fulfilling career outside of the military. Because they loved the military so much, they wonder if they'll ever feel good about their work again.

Negative self-talk bleeds into how you communicate about yourself. If you don't believe you're valuable and worthy, how can you expect someone else to see you that way?

Narrative—How You Speak About Yourself to Others

When you speak and act with confidence, you communicate your value to others. Hesitant job applicants make hiring managers nervous. Confident applicants help employers to envision them already in the job.

What you tell others about yourself has a direct impact on how they describe you. Sounds simple, but it's true. I remember a workshop I ran years ago in which we ran a perception survey on the leadership team in advance of the meeting. When asked to describe the leadership style and views of one executive named Sandy, the feedback respondents universally offered the description of her as "black and white." When I actually met Sandy, she introduced herself as a part of the leadership team, someone who was passionate about the company and its culture and who saw the world simply: as black and white.

The words we tell others about ourselves are the words they'll use to describe us. Tell people that you're a leader with a passion for sustainability, and they'll describe you that way. Tell them you're not very good in social situations, and they'll limit your opportunities to be around groups.

Talking About Your Military Experience

Your military career is a large part of who you are and what you have to offer. But a word of caution here. As you share your experiences with civilian hiring managers and peers, keep in mind that they likely have had limited exposure to the military and will primarily be interested in your experience as it relates to what they are looking for in a job candidate. "For most civilian jobs, no one wants to deal with a professional veteran. They want to work with a veteran who's a professional. There's a big difference," notes Adae Fonseca, Army veteran and corporate veteran advocate. "If it appears you are mentally and emotionally stuck in your time in the service, it could signal a problem to your new employer."

Kevin Preston, a retired Army Colonel who leads veterans programs for a global employer, describes it this way: "Many of the veterans I interview come across almost angry. Angry that civilians don't understand them. Frustrated that their skills don't seem to translate over, they're upset that their new civilian counterparts don't appreciate the career they had before." His advice is to recognize that your career is now outside of the military, away from what you did before, and the colleagues and peers with whom you'll now collaborate have different understandings and experiences to draw on. Yes, you can share your stories and past, but not in a firehose of information, constantly aimed in their direction.

Chris Sanchez, who transitioned from his role as a Navy SEAL to the technology sector, reflects, "I remember when someone in a job interview told me, 'Yes, you were a Navy SEAL then, but what are you now?' It hurt! I expected people to understand the pedigree and what it takes to become a SEAL in the Navy. I expected them to see my value and qualifications as implied. The question stopped me in my tracks and told me that I needed to appreciate my past career, but it was important now to look forward to what comes next."

Narrative—How Others Speak About You

Your narrative reinforces not only how others see you but empowers them to speak about you in the same way. People will talk about you when you aren't present, and you never know who may be able to connect you to a key opportunity. When your network of contacts feels confident they know who you are and what you can offer, they can introduce you to influencers, endorse you publicly, and advocate for your skills, value, and talent. Just like that you've built a sales force who will position you for career opportunities.

Using Your Narrative to Create Your Elevator Pitch

For most people, introducing themselves to a stranger is terrifying. They worry the person will reject them, disregard them, or won't find them interesting or relatable. One way to address this fear is to develop a succinct and compelling elevator pitch.

The term "elevator pitch" or "elevator speech" literally refers to the length of a speech or pitch you can give in the time it takes an elevator to move from the ground floor to the destination. If I turned to you and asked, "What do you do?" or "Tell me about yourself," could you reply with something succinct and interesting enough that I'd want to keep talking with you after the elevator doors open?

To be effective, an elevator pitch needs to share enough about who you are and what you do that the other person is interested and a conversation ensues.

Your elevator pitch is what you will use to introduce yourself at job fairs, networking receptions, job interviews, social events, professional and industry events, and literally in elevators. Whenever someone wants to meet you, it's a great time to share your elevator pitch.

Although you want to make sure you deliver the right message, this is not a script. Your goal is to sound natural and relatable, not robotic or formulaic. Your elevator pitch should contain the following key ingredients, preferably in this order:

1 Your name

2 What you do in nonmilitary language. (You can't assume the other person understands what it means to be an artillery specialist.)

3 Something interesting about yourself, or the reasons why you enjoy your work, or a unique aspect of the work you do

4 What you're looking to do next

Your elevator pitch could sound something like this:

> My name is Kris Smith. I spent 10 years in the Army as a medic, working in high-stress trauma environments. The work was meaningful to me because I'm passionate about service and value being able to help people. Today, I'm in graduate school where I'm learning about the business world, as I plan to pursue a career in medical device sales after graduation.

or

> My name is Mary Jones. After a wonderful career in the Air Force, where I traveled the world as a communications specialist, I'm using those skills to pursue a civilian career in public relations. I love helping companies or individuals tell compelling stories and look forward to doing that for big companies through an agency.

Notice how focused and succinct these examples are. There are many things the recipient of this pitch could follow up on and ask about. That's the point.

Some rules for elevator pitches include:

- **Don't read your resume or recite your life story.** Think short and focused (strive for 60-90 seconds.)

- **Sound natural, not robotic, scripted, or overly rehearsed.**

- **Avoid sharing too much information.** This is a first meeting, not a group therapy session. Keep the conversation succinct.

- **Be careful about using military lingo, jargon, and acronyms.** The odds are you're speaking to a civilian. (The number of civilians versus veterans/active duty service members confirms this.) Your civilian listener will have no idea what you're speaking of if you list your MOS.

- **Smile and maintain good eye contact.** Look at the person when you speak to them. Show that you are approachable.

Your elevator pitch may feel unnatural at first. Practice in front of a mirror and with a friend. Also, you can have multiple, evolving versions of your pitch. If you're on a military base, you can use your acronyms and lingo; chances are, the audience will understand. You can have one version of your elevator pitch that is more formal for use at networking events and job fairs and another that is more relaxed for social events.

As you get comfortable with your elevator pitch, you empower others to help you. Once they know who you are, what you do, and what you're looking for, people can refer you, endorse you, and support you.

At the end of your elevator pitch, remember to ask the other person about themselves. If you neglect to show interest in the person you're speaking to, they may feel that you are only interested in promoting yourself. This can seriously impact their desire to get to know you better.

Leveraging the Power of Networking

Many reports indicate that upward of 80 percent of civilian jobs are found through in-person or online networking. (See the article by Lou Adler at www.linkedin.com/pulse/new-survey-reveals-85-all-jobs-filled-via-networking-lou-adler/.) Networking is the easiest way to promote your successes and strategically put you in the same room with decision makers and influencers who can change your life and career. Your network can become the most powerful part of your military-to-civilian transition.

What Is Networking?

Networking is not about passing out business cards or paying for expensive lunches. Networking is a professional practice where individuals share information and resources and socialize for mutual benefit, with the operative term being "mutual benefit." To be effective, networking must be rewarding for both parties.

Think of it as relationship building. Each of you in a networking relationship needs to be clear about what you can offer and what you need from the other person. As with any relationship, you want reciprocity but not necessarily quid pro quo. For example, I might network with you because you're looking for a job, but that doesn't mean I need your help finding a job. Many of the veterans I've coached tell me, "I have nothing to offer! I just left the military." But it's important to recognize that not everyone needs the same thing in return for their help. Sometimes it's enough to just be appreciative. For instance, if you are networking with a senior professional in the company you'd love to work for and the person provides you with introductions and informational interviews, you could offer to write that person a recommendation on LinkedIn, or send a handwritten thank-you note, or mail a book the person mentioned, or take the person to lunch or coffee. The list goes on. There are many ways to show appreciation for the effort your networking contact provided to you.

Why Is Networking Important?

As you can imagine, networking and relationship building takes time, effort, and attention, but the benefits should outweigh your efforts. Think of networking as building your own sales force. Someone in your network can introduce you to people in their network whom you might otherwise never have had access to. Or they can mention your name to a company that's expanding or walk into a hiring manager's office and recommend you for a position.

Your network can also help you keep informed of unadvertised opportunities as well as important trends and events within your industry. Keeping informed about the latest developments gives you an advantage as you research new jobs or companies. Your network can provide introductions to people in their networks that you might otherwise have a tough time meeting.

What Successful Networking Looks Like

Frank Handoe (USA, Ret.) landed his dream job through networking. "With about 12 months until my retirement from the Army," he said, "I focused on the area my family and I would relocate to. Since we had spent time in Washington State and loved it, I began talking to people in the area about opportunities, the climate, lifestyle, jobs, etc. I nurtured those relationships and kept in touch. When I started terminal leave and my family and I moved to Washington, I met up with those same people I'd spoken to on the phone and offered to buy them coffee and thank them for their information, encouragement, and support over all those months."

That's when his networking efforts paid off. "Over coffee, one man I'd been chatting with shared that there was an opportunity coming up in his organization and he thought I'd be a great fit. He walked my resume into his boss and said, 'I've found the guy we need! I've been speaking with him for a while and think his skills, personality and passion for our work would be a great asset.' Then his boss walked my resume over to HR with that same introduction. After a few interviews, I was hired."

Handoe believes his persistence and commitment to networking was the key to his success. "I didn't just reach out and ask for help. I stayed in touch and offered value wherever I could. These people wanted to help me, and I showed my gratitude, which made a positive impression. If you're worried about networking, trust me, it works!"

Who Should Be in Your Network?

Four types of individuals are assets to your network. Each serves different, very specific purposes in your professional growth and development.

1 **Decision makers.** These people are in the position to benefit you directly. If you are looking for a job, you want to have hiring managers and recruiters in your network. If you're starting your own business and looking for funding, you want to network with investors, investment bankers, or other people who have access to capital. Decision makers have the ability to hire or write a check or bring you into the environment where that can happen.

2 **Influencers.** An endorsement from an influencer carries a lot of weight and authority with the people they know. Influencers are well respected and known in the industries or communities they serve.

3 **Information sources.** These people may or may not be decision makers or influencers, but they are extremely knowledgeable about things you're not. For instance, you might seek out expert writers to help you craft your online profiles or specialists in the retail industry if you're interested in a career in retail supply chain. When you meet someone with deep expertise in an area, consider whether the subject area they are expert in is of value to you.

4 **Cheerleaders.** These individuals may be decision makers, influencers, or even information sources, but they are also optimistic, encouraging, and supportive. Your network needs to include people who lift you up and provide support throughout your career. As you meet these people, include them in your network for those times when you need professional encouragement.

How to Get Started in Building Your Network

To begin building your network, follow these steps:

1 **List who you know.** Write down the names of the people you know. You might consider leaving close family off your list. Although I don't like to network with family over holiday dinners, if you do, put their names down. Add the names of people you have kept in touch with from high school and college as well as colleagues and coworkers from any jobs you've had, on base or off. Be sure to also include people you've met through your volunteer work or at job search events, such as job fairs, gatherings, and meetups.

2 **Catalog your contacts and add labels.** Organize your contacts into a searchable program like Microsoft Excel or Word. You might categorize and label them by how you know them, what you know about them, how long you've known them, any opportunities or challenges they could potentially present for you. You should also give each contact a label that's helpful to you, such as "decision maker" or "influencer." This enables you to search for all the influencers you know in a company when you need advocates to walk your resume into the hiring team.

3 **Touch base with the people you've listed.** If you haven't been in touch for a while, send an email or note online to reintroduce yourself and reestablish contact. Remind them how you know them and what you're up to now. It's OK to be brief. For example, you might send the following note:

> It's been a few years since we met in biology lab at U.C.L.A. I remember how much I enjoyed working with you on our senior project. I hope things are going well for you.
>
> I'm getting ready to exit my career in the Coast Guard and will be relocating back to the Los Angeles area. Are you still in town? It would be great to reconnect and meet for coffee sometime. I look forward to hearing back from you and seeing you again.

4 **Make a list of who you need to know.** As you inventory your existing contacts, you'll likely see areas where you need to know more people. Perhaps most of your contacts are fellow soldiers, and you would like to know more professionals in finance. Or maybe your contacts are all military, and you're seeking more civilian relationships. Start to make lists of categories of people you need to know, such as experts in financial services, personal branding specialists, or professionals with contacts in higher education. Write down any individual names you've identified as potential good contacts. Are there people whose names keep coming up in conversation as good for you to know? When you watch the news, are there industry experts who could help you learn about trends and happenings? Is there a hiring manager in your dream company whom you would love to connect with? Make lists of these people too.

5 **See where you can connect the dots.** After you've made the list of who you know and how you know them and have identified who you need or want to know, see where you can connect the people you already know to the people you wish to know. Tools like LinkedIn are a tremendous asset here. On LinkedIn, you can enter the name of an individual or company you'd like to be connected to, and the system will tell you all the ways you are already linked. For instance, if you'd like to meet the hiring manager at your dream company, LinkedIn can tell you if anyone in your network has worked at that company, currently works there, or knows that hiring manager.

6 **Start thinking of ways you can reciprocate.** Right now you're likely in the phase of searching for what you need, but remember that networking is a two-way street. As you identify people you know or wish to know, consider how you could help them. Do they seek to know more about the military? Do they do work with the branch of service you're leaving? Are they looking to grow their network of contacts? What do they need and how can you help them?

Maintaining Your Networking Relationships

One of the most disappointing and ungratifying aspects of networking is when you help someone find a job, make a valuable connection, or refer them to an opportunity, and they take the offer and then vanish from contact. This happens way too often to be an anomaly and may dissuade a networking contact from offering similar support to someone else in the future.

Be sure to maintain your networking relationships, whether you find a job quickly or it takes time. When you are introduced to a new connection, circle back to your original contact and not only thank them but update them on the conversation. Let them know whether that introduction produced something valuable, and remind them that you appreciate their support.

You should also maintain your network relationships in case the job or opportunity you secure doesn't work out. If you need more assistance later but failed to stay in touch with someone who helped you, they may be less inclined to help you in the future.

As you nurture and maintain these relationships, seek new ways to connect with your contacts. If your contact has been primarily on LinkedIn, is it time to talk by phone? If you have been emailing back and forth for months and live in the same area, can you meet for coffee? It is a small way to take the relationship further, but it adds a more personal touch, which deepens your connection.

Don't forget to check in with your contacts and see how you can help them. Right now, you are focused on getting what you need, but your networking contacts have needs too. Check in on their career, goals, needs, growth plans—how can you help?

Where Can You Network?

Worried about where to meet these amazing people? The good news is you can meet them anywhere, from standing in line for a coffee, to sitting next to them on an airplane, to having your kids play for the same soccer team, to job fairs, corporate open houses and hiring events, meetups, and everywhere in between. You can meet networking contacts anywhere.

Job Fairs

Also known as career expos or career fairs, job fairs will likely play a role in your transition to a civilian career. Job fairs provide the opportunity for a group of employers to share their programs, job openings, career options, and company highlights. Job fairs may also feature presentations, seminars, workshops, and perhaps opportunities to meet one-on-one with employers, mentors, or coaches who can help with interview techniques, resume review, social media profiles, and other aspects of the transition.

The purpose of a job fair is to introduce and connect employers with job seekers who might be eligible for open positions within their company. Ideally every employer at a military-to-civilian job fair has open positions that a veteran could reasonably qualify to fill, has veterans manning their booth (or at least brings civilian team members who are versed on the military experience), and is interested in meeting applicants for their company. This is not always the case, however. Sometimes employers attend and exhibit at job fairs to "wave the flag" and introduce the applicant job pool to their company and what they do. This can be a frustrating experience for those attending the job fair believing that every employer is ready to hire someone like them.

Research the Companies

Preparation and research are critical steps for a successful job fair experience. Before you attend your first job fair, I recommend the following:

- Research the employers that will be in attendance and identify those that interest you.

- Look at the company website, online articles, and other media sites to learn about the company values, mission and purpose.

- Identify those companies whose values align with yours and narrow your focus to these employers.

- Study the company's history and business projections and understand how they are positioned against their market competitors.

With a list of targeted employers in hand, review open positions at these companies. Look on the "careers" pages of the company website, cross-reference open jobs on sites like Indeed.com or Monster.com to see what positions are open currently, and check what it takes to be qualified to fill them.

Then modify your resume, wardrobe, and elevator pitch to reflect the needs and wants of the desired employer. You want to look and sound like someone who understands the company and would fit in. You may also wish to bring along other support materials to help the hiring process move forward.

Advance research is critical before attending a job fair. Employers are looking for candidates who are focused, informed, and specific about what they want, how they can add value, and why this company is a match. Employers want candidates who make it easy for them by researching who they are and what they need in advance.

Set a Game Plan

With your research in hand, approaching a job fair should be a strategic endeavor. Before you head out the door, plan your time there, who you want to meet, what you want to learn, how you'll communicate your value, and what needs to happen for you to consider the job fair a success. Consider these questions to develop your job fair game plan:

- **What five to seven companies do you want to meet with?** How will you approach them? Which open jobs there will you apply for? Do you know anything about the recruiters or company team members who may be on site? What information will you share about yourself to stand out? How will you ensure a positive impression?

- **What on-site programs, seminars, or workshops will you attend?** What do you hope to learn from them? Will you connect with the presenter in advance or afterward? How will you leverage what you've learned to build your career?

- **What time will you arrive and what time will you leave the job fair?** Thinking about this in advance prevents you from leaving too early or arriving late.

- **How will you get to the event?** This might sound like a simple question, but if you aren't sure where to park or don't know which train or bus to take, you could arrive flustered and frustrated. Plan every step as best you can in advance.

- **What materials will you bring?** In a portfolio or manila envelope, bring clean copies of your resume (if more than one page, be sure to staple them in advance). Will you also bring business cards, lists of references, or additional information? Be sure to carry them in a pouch or briefcase to keep them clean and neat.

- **Who else would you like to meet?** There will be many job seekers, employers, presenters, event hosts, and others in attendance with you. Which of them would you like to meet? Do you want to meet with other job seekers who are leaving your same duty station at the same time? Those meetings could lead to friendships, collaboration, and even sharing of resources as you move through your process of building a civilian career.

- **What's your elevator pitch?** What makes you valuable to the companies you want to approach? What about your background, passions, skills, and talents aligns with their hiring goals?

- **Did you spend time reviewing your resume?** Whether you wrote it yourself or you had help, be sure you can speak to everything listed on your resume. Ensure it is sufficiently demilitarized to be relatable to civilian hiring managers and recruiters and that the language, tone, and results listed are yours and are consistent with what you represent in person.

- **What will you do to keep yourself positive?** Job fairs are hard work and can be exhausting. No matter how frustrated or tired you feel, greet every new person with a smile, a firm handshake, and a positive attitude. The next person you meet may be the exact person you need for a great new career. If need be, build in extra time between meetings to get some fresh air and regroup emotionally.

Introducing Yourself: Approaching a Stranger

Does the idea of introducing yourself to strangers over and over and over again at a job fair intimidate or frustrate you? I shared my some of my favorite tips for introducing yourself to strangers in an article on Military.com (www.military.com/veteran-jobs/career-advice/job-hunting/how-to-introduce-yourself-to-a-stranger.html). Here are the highlights.

In the civilian world, there are many instances when you will need to introduce yourself to someone new, whether it is a business meeting, career fair, community gathering, or job interview. Follow these steps for meeting someone new to ensure a positive impression:

1 **Take the initiative.** When walking into a room of strangers, most people stand off to the side and assess the landscape: Who's there, who looks friendly and approachable, and where's the exit? For this reason, at most events, you see a line of people pressed against the wall, heads down looking at their smartphone, or hugging onto a high-top table for dear life. Instead, walk to the middle of the room with confidence. Assess the situation in terms of whom you should meet, who looks interesting, and who you will initiate conversation with. Since most of the attendees will be hesitant to introduce themselves to strangers, when you project confidence and certainty, you make it easier for them to talk to you. Make it your job to put others at ease by taking the initiative and introducing yourself.

2 **Shake hands.** When meeting someone new, extend your hand for a greeting. An approachable person shakes hands to convey warmth, friendliness, and confidence. Resist the temptation to squeeze their hand into submission. A bone-crushing handshake is not enjoyable and leaves a negative impression. Similarly, don't offer a wet-fish handshake that is weak and limp. This leaves the impression of low confidence and self-worth.

3 **Make eye contact.** When you look someone in the eyes, you show them that you are present and ready to converse. For many people, eye contact feels too intimate, so they look off to the side when speaking to someone they don't know. Imagine how that feels for the other person. Awkward. Good eye contact displays your humanity and enables you to read the other person's body language. Are they afraid? Are they happy? Are they distracted? If you watch their eye contact cues, you can adjust your body language and words to support or confirm what they need.

4 **Ask, then listen.** When feeling anxious, many people tend to talk too much and monopolize the conversation. When you do all the talking and don't ask questions, the other person becomes bored and uninterested. Remember that you are at an event to make connections and ask questions in order to find out about career opportunities. Be sure to ask open-ended questions to solicit conversational responses. For instance, if you ask, "Do you like networking events?," you'll receive a yes or no answer. Instead, if you ask, "What do you find most valuable from this kind of event?," you will receive an answer that starts a conversation.

5 Let them go (when it's time). When is it time to say good-bye to a new contact? If you've been talking to someone who is painfully shy and afraid to talk to new people, they might not want to end the conversation with you because then they are alone again. If your goal is to meet new people, then it's unfair to you to stay in one conversation for an extended period. Graciously wrap up the conversation when you feel there is little left to discuss, or your interest is waning, or you wish to talk to other people. Politely say, "I've really enjoyed talking with you and look forward to continuing the conversation later. I'll email you to set up a time to grab coffee." Then say good-bye. Only say this if you truly do intend to follow up. If not, then offer something like "Thank you for spending time telling me about your long career. I'm sure you'd like to meet other people here too, so I'll say good-bye for now."

Someone who confidently approaches strangers, introduces themselves, and ends the conversation gracefully leaves a positive impression. Most of the people you meet are just as intimidated about meeting you as you are to meet them.

Following Up

Follow up with the employers, speaker/trainers, or attendees you met at the job fair. Be sure to get their business cards, and immediately after meeting the person, jot notes on the back of their card or on a separate notepad, so you can remember what to mention when you contact them later. For example, if you met a recruiter and discussed your common interest in landscape photography (even if that's unrelated to the job), mention it in your follow-up so the recruiter can more easily remember who you were. Just like you, each person you meet at a job fair is meeting many other people. As much as you can identify something specific and unique that you discussed with them, the easier it will be to remember you.

Follow-up by email. If there was something you promised to do quickly, such as send a list of references, send additional information about your background, or set up an in-person interview, follow up on that as soon as you leave the job fair.

If there was no immediate or obvious follow-up, still do so. You could send an email after the job fair thanking the person for their time speaking with you. Refer back to the conversation and indicate a next step, such as keeping an eye on their Careers page on the website, checking back in a few months, or following up on a lead they provided.

Tools to Use for In-Person Networking

Although you can network without these tools, having them certainly helps.

- **Business cards** with your name, phone number, and email address make it easy for someone to contact you after meeting you. You can also include a link to your online profiles or website, if you have them.
- Your **elevator pitch** should be refined and well rehearsed before you set out to meet professional contacts. You need to clearly, concisely, and confidently communicate who you are, what you do, and what you're looking for.
- **Online profiles** are very helpful to your networking contacts. Having a polished LinkedIn profile makes it easy for someone to find you, read more about your experience and skills, and refer you to others.

In Closing

How you speak about yourself tells others whether you have confidence, direction, and goals. Refrain from negative self-talk and feed yourself positive affirmations to keep your spirits high during this time of transition.

Then, as you venture out to network, remember you are relationship building. Yes, the relationships must be mutually beneficial and have career value to you, but they can still be engaging, informative, and enjoyable.

Narrative and networking are tools you'll use today, tomorrow, and for the remainder of your life. Think about the long game here: Being able to articulate who you are and what you can offer and then building strategic and valuable relationships that reward you with contacts, referrals, and insight gives you the building blocks for long-term career growth.

Getting Yourself Out There

07

Networking Online

Social media and social networks are powerful places to elevate, enhance, and build your personal brand and reputation. Although there are risks with posting personal information online, the benefits can be compelling. Your online connections learn what you are passionate about, they see consistent evidence of your values and skills, and you remain "top of mind," positioning you well for a key opportunity.

Statistics reinforce the position that an online presence is a necessity for a 21st-century professional:

- Personal referrals are five times more effective than all other sources of hiring. When someone refers you for an opportunity, they will likely link to your online profile.[1]

- At more than 38 percent of the American workforce, millennials are using social networking to build their brands and promote themselves. By 2025, they will make up 75 percent of the workforce, driving the importance and ease of social networking to help employers evaluate job applicants.[2]

- About 95 percent of external recruiters rely on LinkedIn to find candidates to present to their client companies seeking top-tier talent.[3]

- 70 percent of employers review social media sites to screen and evaluate candidates before hiring, and about 43 percent of employers use social media to check on current employees.[4]

- As you navigate your military-to-civilian career transition, consider whether you can risk not being found online by employers, whether your reputation is suffering from what you've posted, and how you can elevate your positioning with a strong online presence.

How to Be Authentic Online Without Sharing Everything

Since we know that people connect with and do business with people they like, it's important to show your humanity and authenticity to others online. A common struggle among social media users is sharing enough so people find you relatable but not sharing so much that you make people uncomfortable or are seen as "oversharing." There's always that one Facebook friend or Instagram connection who shares too many details.

Sharing on social media should be filtered through the lens of authenticity. When you post, comment, share an image, or "like" something online, you are letting others see who you are, what you value, and where your passions lie. You tell them what's important to you, what you believe in, what you like (and don't like), and where you focus your energy.

There are no written rules or published guidelines on how to communicate authenticity online. I encourage you to ask yourself the next questions to ensure you are projecting the values of your personal brand but not oversharing.

- **Am I holding back because I'm afraid of being judged?** Others will naturally judge you; it's human nature. When you are clear on your personal brand, you are purposefully driving the impression and affecting the judgment others will form of you. Don't let judgment from others hold you back from sharing your views, opinions, and insights where they strengthen your value in your career.

- **Am I sharing information that helps others learn who I am?** Sharing your latest dinner creation may not tell others much about your value as a manager, but sharing your passion for helping people through your volunteer work will.

- **Could this post, photo, share, or comment hurt me later?** A candid photo of you enjoying a family barbecue with several empty beer bottles lined up next to you could indicate your ability to relax but might be a red flag to a future employer who questions your judgment in posting such an image.

- **Am I willing to discuss what I've posted?** To share something online and then refuse to engage in conversation or debate over your post is unfair. Someone who posts a controversial political opinion yet disables comments or refuses to discuss why they feel the way they do frustrates online users. Be willing and ready to continue any conversation you initiate or participate in online.

Thinking intentionally and strategically about what you share, comment on, and post is critical. Too often, online users are careless or hurried about posting and find themselves in trouble afterwards. Consider these scenarios:

- Bob, a job applicant, posts photos of himself smashing his MacBook Pro laptop on Facebook after the computer failed to boot up again. A year later, Bob applies to work at the Genius Bar in the local Apple Store. The interviewer does a scan of Bob's social media accounts and sees the rant, disqualifying him.

- Susan is thrilled that her colleague, Amy, is finally pregnant. They've worked alongside each other for years, and Susan knows of Amy and her husband's struggle to conceive. In her excitement and job, Susan shares a "shout out" of congratulations to Amy on Facebook, not realizing Amy hadn't told their employer yet. Now Amy is in a challenging position and fears a big project could be taken away from her.

- An offhand comment, off-color joke, insensitive online post, or explicitly racist, sexist, or discriminatory share can cause someone to lose friends, connections, clients, jobs, or even career choices. What happens online is public.

If you fear that something you might have shared or posted previously could become a problem, the good news is you can remove it. Untag yourself from images or posts that are inappropriate and remove posts, comments, and shares that could cause viewers to question you and your integrity.

Which Platform Do You Start With?

Not all social networking sites function the same way or serve the same purpose. A look at the top social networking platforms will help you decide where to start.

Facebook

I admit I really didn't understand Facebook when I first saw it. My high school–aged sons were constantly connected to Facebook, watching funny videos, seeing what their friends were posting, and keeping tabs on their favorite professional athletes. Beyond that, I didn't understand the point of Facebook. Over time, however, I learned that Facebook is the more social side of social networking.

Many of you may have found Facebook to be a valuable tool for connection, sharing, camaraderie, and keeping in touch during your time in the military. Many service members post content onto Facebook to "keep morale and spirits high" and to update families back home on their deployment.

Facebook can serve many valuable functions in your post-military career. You can share the more personal or social side of your personal brand and your career aspirations. You can link and connect with causes, issues, people, and companies that align with your values and passions. Many of the companies you'll research as potential employers have Facebook business pages, which are great places to see how the company interacts in a more candid, social, and relaxed way. You can learn a lot about a company's culture through their Facebook page.

It's important to remember that what you post on Facebook should be assumed to be "public," regardless of privacy settings. Anyone you're connected to can share, take a screenshot of, or otherwise promote your images, connections, content, and opinions. Facebook is not a safe place to let your most intimate feelings show, believing them to be private.

Twitter

Twitter can be described as user-generated content on steroids. With Twitter's looser rules and guidelines, Twitter users share everything on their minds, constantly. It can feel like an unmanageable firehose of content streaming unless you filter and drive content into themes or lists or use hashtags. Twitter can be an excellent place to follow trends, events, and news from industries, companies, or influential leaders you care about.

Instagram

Instagram is the most visual of the social networking platforms. Users on Instagram post images, photos, graphics, videos, memes, and other content with a description attached. Users can post hashtags to help other users find content that is tagged by location, topic, subject matter, or subject. For users who prefer to communicate through photos, images, graphics, videos, and other visual mediums, Instagram is great.

LinkedIn

LinkedIn is considered by many to be a key social networking site for professional conversations.

LinkedIn offers members a free platform on which they can build individual profiles and showcase their experience, skills, successes, and promotional materials. Members connect with other members and begin collaborations. Some LinkedIn connections never transfer to in-person connections, but others do. Such transfers are not assumed.

As a member of the civilian workforce, you will want to establish a professional presence on LinkedIn. Often a new contact will look to LinkedIn to see what they can learn about your work background and credentials. An employer may review your LinkedIn profile to see how you present yourself online. Your current employer may view your LinkedIn profile to see where you received your certifications. A networking contact may look at your LinkedIn profile to see what you look like, as they wait to meet you at the coffee shop.

LinkedIn also offers several powerful career and networking tools.

- LinkedIn allows members to contact each other on the site, with some limitations. You can directly email LinkedIn members to whom you are connected.

- LinkedIn Groups allow members to interact with each other over a topic or area of interest. For instance, there are a LinkedIn Groups of Air Force Veterans, Project Management Professionals, Artists in the Seattle Area, and hundreds of others. Groups encourage members to learn from others; share insights, opinions, or information with connections or potential connections; and learn what topics are trending and timely.

- Articles posted by professionals online allow other connections to learn about developments or trends in that professional's industry, new research and insight into their company or profession, and reveal more about the author to their target audience.

Here are ten things to do now to elevate your profile and ensure successful engagement on LinkedIn:

1   **Clarify what you're looking for.** As you approach your exit from the military and become clearer about what you want to do next (and where), update your LinkedIn profile. Turn on the button on your profile that indicates you are "Open to Opportunities," maybe state that in your About section, and put an end date in the description of your current job. This tells recruiters and hiring managers that you are ready to be sourced and hired.

2   **Follow influencers.** There are many well-known and influential people on LinkedIn. From Jeff Weiner, former CEO of LinkedIn, to Brené Brown, a Texas-based researcher who has created speeches and business tools around the topic of courage and vulnerability, many people on LinkedIn can inspire and influence your career going forward.

3   **Follow target companies.** The site allows you to "follow" up to 1,000 companies so make it your goal to follow any company

you're even possibly interested in. Look at the industry categories of your target career—who are the leaders in that industry? Who are the up-and-coming companies? Whose work and business do you admire and seek to learn more about? When you follow these companies on LinkedIn, their updates, announcements, and posts will appear in your feed, giving you the opportunity to learn about any job openings, business changes, or challenges quickly so you can respond.

4   **Fill out every box.** LinkedIn offers you several areas and opportunities to expand your story. Take full advantage of every chance to showcase your expertise, highlight your skills, and explain your value. Your profile will indicate where you might have information missing, tell you how complete the profile is, and even offer suggestions for improving the profile's impact.

5   **List your military employer.** Under "last (or current) employer," list the branch of service you are transitioning from so that the logo of that branch (US Coast Guard, US Army, etc.) appears. This enables recruiters who search for veterans on LinkedIn to find you more easily.

6   **Share content.** It is not enough to build a profile and connect to other people. The purpose of the site is to collaborate and share information, resources, and insight. If you're concerned that you don't know what to post, consider sharing updates on your transition. Keep in mind that hiring managers and recruiters can see what you post, so make sure what you post serves you well. Consider posting articles or links to videos that speak to your career interests and goals.

7   **Check the site daily.** Make looking at what's happening in your network part of your routine at the start of your day, at lunch, or in the evening. Comment on or share posts that interest you, relate to your career goals, or help build your reputation.

8   **Become active in LinkedIn Groups.** LinkedIn Groups form around topics, causes, industries, and even companies. You might look for groups around your military service. For instance, if you are leaving the Marine Corps, you can enter "Marine Corps" into the LinkedIn search bar, and it will return a

long list of groups related to that topic. Various associations, support groups, and networks might be helpful to you. Consider groups that focus on transition (i.e., the Veterans Mentor Network on LinkedIn has over 137,000 members in 2019). Also explore other areas, such as industry-focused groups, to show employers that you are ready to join a post-military community.

Once you have found a few groups that interest you, start reading through the online conversations. If those threads interest you, contribute your ideas, thoughts, or suggestions and begin to build relationships with other group participants. If a group isn't posting content you find valuable, helpful, or interesting, leave it and find another one. Since it's important to participate in the groups you belong to, keep this list manageable.

9 **Mind the optics of your profile.** Look at your LinkedIn profile as a recruiter might. If they landed on your page, what would they see? Would they see a military-heavy profile, with loads of military acronyms and language unrelatable outside of the military? Would they see someone who is connected only to other service members, who follows only military organizations, and is active only in veteran-focused groups? Employers appreciate your desire to connect with others who've served and stay part of that community as you go forward, but show them that you are focused on jobs, companies, and industries that will serve you in your next career.

10 **Update when appropriate.** Posting to your LinkedIn network too often can be overwhelming to your connections. Similarly, if you never post, it's easy to forget you're there. Strive to post regularly and make sure the content is valuable and appropriate to the people who follow you.

Build Relationships That Serve You Too

Across all social media sites and social networking platforms, if you are mindful and intentional about the people you connect with, they will serve you over the course of your career. You can certainly connect with family and friends on Facebook and Instagram, but when it comes to relationships outside of your close circle of supporters, seek connections that can turn into mutually beneficial professional relationships.

On all sites, I'm connected to business colleagues, clients, media contacts, friends, family members, advocates, supporters, influencers, and teammates of my company. Being purposeful about each relationship empowers me to know how to serve them and how they can serve me. For some, I may have a direct request ("Can you introduce me to Joe Smith at ABC Company?"); for others the request may be more subtle ("If you like this article, please share it with your network"); and for others I may just request they think about something I've posted or join me in celebrating a success. Each of these contacts serves a purpose for me, and I return that favor for them, often and publicly.

Choosing Your Online Connections

Social networking is still networking, which means that it's about relationships. Every new online contact you have should meet the same criteria as your in-person contacts. If you can't develop a mutually beneficial professional relationship with an online contact, that contact shouldn't be in your network.

I'm very particular about whom I'll connect with online. In my view, when I connect with someone online, I'm introducing that new contact to my existing network of contacts, which gives this new connection access to my network. Consider what would happen if my new LinkedIn connection began spamming my contacts with sales messages or using their new relationship with me as credibility for their pushiness? That can damage my online reputation and personal brand.

Online networking has a scalability element that's unreachable in person. We can communicate with thousands of contacts through a post, update, or online article, whereas that might be hard to do in person, one contact at a time.

Although it is infinitely more scalable than in-person networking, online networking should similarly not be seen as a way to "hide" behind the keyboard. People you connect with online still want to know that a real person is building a professional relationship with them online.

Sending Requests to Connect

If you were to approach a stranger at a networking event, would you hand them your business card and not say anything, hoping they would accept it and begin speaking to you? Certainly not. Yet people do this on LinkedIn all the time. They send invitations to connect to complete strangers, expecting to start a mutually rewarding professional relationship.

Whenever possible, personalize the invitation to connect before you send it. Help the recipient understand why you want to be part of their network. Maybe you know them from someplace, or they've written something you found interesting or important. Perhaps you see an opportunity to help them, or you share common connections, interests, experiences, or goals.

When you personalize the invitation to connect, you increase the likelihood your request will be reviewed and accepted. There still may be reasons someone doesn't connect with you; try not to take that personally. Some people do not accept LinkedIn connections where there could be a potential conflict of interest, such as if they work at a competing company. Others do not check their email or LinkedIn profile often enough to manage incoming requests.

Accepting Requests to Connect

When you receive a request to connect on LinkedIn that is not personalized, evaluate the opportunity (or risk) from various angles:

- Do you know this person (is their name familiar?) If you know them, do you see a benefit from connecting? Is there any risk to connecting?

- If you don't know this person, click to view their LinkedIn profile. Do you see any commonalities there? Did you serve in the same branch of the military, attend the same school, or grow up near each other? Do you share multiple contacts in common, and are these contacts you know well?

- Is there something in their career experience, skills set, or volunteer experiences that intrigues or interests you? Perhaps you've been interested in a career in physical therapy and just enrolled in online classes, and they are trained as a PT. Maybe that is why they wanted to connect with you.

- Are you members of the same group on LinkedIn? This could indicate shared experience or interest. You might recognize them from comments or posts they made in the group.

Why Recommendations Matter on LinkedIn

LinkedIn offers two direct ways your connections can endorse and promote you to their network and support you on your profile: recommendations and endorsements. Endorsements come in the form of clicking a button next to various skills you list, showing that they support your claim of expertise and knowledge in that skill. With or without even direct knowledge of who you are and how you work, someone can endorse your skills if they are connected to you on the site.

Recommendations, in contrast, require more work and must be attached to someone with an active LinkedIn profile, which gives recommendations more credibility. A viewer of your profile can click through to see the background of the person offering the recommendation, increasing its value to your profile.

Recommendations offer you the chance to highlight aspects of your hard or soft skills that might be awkward for you to list. For instance, if your experience paints the picture of someone who thrives on intense situations, who's handled high-profile crisis and traveled extensively, and you'd like people to know that you have a great sense of humor and know how to balance work and life, those attributes can be highlighted in a recommendation by someone who worked closely with you and saw you that way.

Action

As you build your online profiles, ensure you are:

☐ **Presenting yourself strategically.** Think about the impression you want to make with the audiences you'll attract.

☐ **Evaluating each online platform for its usefulness in your career strategy.** All platforms are not the same. Consider the audience you seek to attract, and where that audience participates online.

☐ **Showing consistency across all social media sites.** While Facebook is more casual and social, and LinkedIn is more professional, your connections should see aspects of the same person. Consistency is critical.

☐ **Evaluating which platforms return the best results for your career goals.** Facebook could provide you more feedback and support, while Twitter gives you breaking news that keeps your competitive edge, and LinkedIn connects you to influencers and decision makers you need to grow your career. If a platform no longer serves you, consider whether you need to maintain your effort there.

☐ **Connecting and engaging with others.** Start a conversation with your new connection by mentioning something about their work, your goals, or a common interest. Over time, support them by commenting on their posts, sharing their ideas, and celebrating their successes.

In Closing

The world of social networking might feel too risky or unmanageable at the outset. There is a lot to learn about positioning yourself to get the right attention from the right contacts and make a positive impression. But if you start slow and build your online presence intentionally and strategically, the cost of time invested returns great rewards.

Whether you'll pursue education, entrepreneurship, or employment after the military, social networking likely will play a crucial role in your ability to gather information, learn about trends and happenings, and connect with individuals who can help you and whom you can support.

Notes

1 Ronen Shetelboim, "2017 Recruiting Funnel Benchmark Report Now Available," Jobvite Blog, May 4, 2017, www.jobvite.com/jobvite-news-and-reports/2017-recruiting-funnel-benchmark-report-now-available/ (archived at https://perma.cc/B9YP-XHBT)

2 Gallup 2016 Report, *How Millennials Want to Work and Live*, www. gallup.com/workplace/238073/millennials-work-live.aspx (archived at https://perma.cc/6LCK-2XKU)

3 Marcelle Yeager, "How to Get Replies to Your Messages on LinkedIn," *U.S. News & World Report,* April 20, 2017, https://money.usnews.com/money/blogs/outside-voices-careers/articles/2017-04-20/how-to-get-replies-to-your-messages-on-linkedin (archived at https://perma.cc/H6PM-2C7X)

4 "More Than Half of Employers Have Found Content on Social Media That Caused Them NOT to Hire a Candidate, According to Recent CareerBuilder Survey," CareerBuilder, August 9, 2018, https://www.prnewswire.com/news-releases/more-than-half-of-employers-have-found-content-on-social-media-that-caused-them-not-to-hire-a-candidate-according-to-recent-careerbuilder-survey-300694437.html (archived at https://perma.cc/R7D6-VNLK)

Finding Mentors, Apprenticeships, and Internships

08

Each of us during our career needs help. During those times, wouldn't it be nice to have access to an individual who is farther along in their career, has a network of contacts, sees the world in a new, different, or better way than you, is supportive and encouraging, and is willing to help you for no cost? That's what it means to have a mentor.

The mentee is the one who receives the mentoring, and the mentor is the individual who volunteers time and expertise to provide guidance, access to resources, information, or support. On-the-job mentoring can produce deeper understanding of your work and expectations, better connectedness to the company and your career, and a feeling of support and encouragement as you build your skills and experience.

Today, there are numerous formal and informal opportunities for mentoring before, and after, you leave the military and as you grow your civilian career. According to Daniel Rau (USMC), cofounder and chief executive of Veterati.com, a digital mentorship platform for the military community, most military people come to mentoring for (in this order) advice around their career, branding and self-marketing, transition assistance, and guidance on entrepreneurship. Rau also notes that mentoring is growing as a career tool for everyone. "Navigating transition is not just a military experience, it's a human experience. Veterans can certainly benefit from mentoring with professionals who also face inflection points in their professional and personal journeys and can share that experience and knowledge with the military community."

Finding a Mentor

Although there are formal programs that match suitable mentors with mentees, sometimes you might need to find mentor on your own. Your personal and professional networks can provide you with leads for finding a mentor who matches up with what you are looking for.

LinkedIn is a great place to identify someone with the passion, skills, and insights you seek. You might even find someone in your local community who is highly regarded for their talents and willingness to help others.

Remember that asking someone to mentor you requires them to realize a benefit as well. Just because you need the help doesn't mean someone is inclined to offer it. You need to lay some groundwork first. Get to know them and let them see who you are and what you're committed to. Help them to see how the relationship will benefit them. When a possible mentor feels that their investment of time, resources, insight, and support will be well served with you, they'll likely be receptive to the idea.

Leveraging a Mentoring Program

Finding someone qualified and willing to mentor you is easier today than ever before. There are companies designed to connect veterans to civilian mentors, community programs that sponsor connection and collaboration, and many organizations that offer both formal and informal mentorship programs.

Two of the most popular mentoring platforms for veterans are American Corporate Partners (ACP) and Veterati.com.

American Corporate Partners was founded in 2008 to connect veterans and military spouses with mentors who can provide career and transition guidance. ACP provides veterans with the opportunity to connect with guides to achieve typical mentorship goals, such as:

- Preparing for an interview
- Exploring careers and understanding job opportunities
- Helping with career advancement once a position is obtained
- Establishing work-life balance

- Learning how to network
- Developing your small business
- Professional communications

Mentors and mentees make a one-year commitment with monthly calls to ensure that goals and objectives are met and tracked. Each relationship is monitored and supported by an ACP staff member, who provides valuable resources and guidance to ensure the relationship produces successful outcomes for the veteran mentee.

In January 2016, Veterati.com was launched as a web-based mentoring solution connecting service members, veterans, and military spouses to mentors for on-demand mentoring. Veterati.com uses features like algorithmic matching, smart calendar syncing, text messaging notifications, and automated reviews to enhance the user experience.

Under the Veterati.com model, mentee users connect with as many mentors as they find valuable. Users register on the website, complete a profile featuring their areas of interest and expertise, and select mentors (based on their profiles) to connect with. Mentors pre-offer their availability for the month as available meeting slots, and veterans book appointments with their mentor as needed. On the day and time of the meeting, the Veterati.com phone system connects mentor to mentee for a one-hour call. Afterward, the system asks for reviews and evaluations of the call to determine effectiveness and to troubleshoot any issues.

I have been a "super mentor" (meaning I have spent more than 100 hours volunteering mentoring services) on Veterati.com for years. Veterans tell me they like the ease of use of the technology, the reminders from the system about upcoming appointments, and the impact of the coaching they receive from mentors across all stages of career and all industries.

Your Employer May Offer Mentoring

A formal mentoring program inside a company may consist of an application process to be accepted into the program, training for mentors and mentees on leveraging the relationship, regular meetings and check-ins, and even a graduation at the end of the mentoring program.

Informal mentoring can occur when one person seeks regular guidance and coaching from a peer or supervisor with more knowledge, acumen, or insight into the area of growth sought. Whether the program is formal or informal, knowing that someone is invested in your success makes the mentoring relationship mutually rewarding.

Choosing a Mentor

When looking for a mentor, consider how well their skill set, work experience, proximity to you, and willingness to mentor match what you're looking for. Just because you identify someone as a great candidate to support, encourage, coach, and lead you does not mean they have the time, inclination, or desire to mentor you. Someone you might want to mentor you might have other obligations, could already be mentoring someone else, or may be reluctant to mentor you for fear they aren't confident in their skills or abilities. That needs to be okay.

Getting the Most from a Mentor

In order to get the most out of your mentoring relationship, be as clear as possible with your mentor about your goals and objectives. If you want to build a career in finance after leaving the Navy, your mentor needs to know as much as possible about your goals. Which field of financial services do you want to work in? What challenges do you anticipate? What opportunities have you identified? If you communicate your goals and expectations clearly, your mentor can provide you with the right guidance.

From the onset of your mentoring relationship, it's important to allow yourself to be vulnerable. Your mentor is enlisted to help and support you. If their advice is confusing or makes you uncomfortable, tell them. They want to see you succeed, and you can help them by sharing how you feel during and along the process.

Max Dubroff (USAF, Ret.), who works as a human resources specialist and hiring manager, has mentored many veterans in his career and shares this advice for a positive mentoring relationship:

- **Go plural.** Don't just seek out one mentoring relationship but try for a few. This gives you multiple perspectives on the advice you'll receive.

- **Go nonlinear.** Seek mentors who bring completely different backgrounds, experiences, and skills to get a well-rounded perspective.

- **Go now.** Many veterans wait for what they think is the right time and wait too long. Find a mentor now.

- **Go thoughtfully.** Be considerate about whom you ask and where you need guidance. Ask good questions to understand their perspective on your question.

Dubroff advises his mentees to be honest and to accept honest feedback. "If the mentor is concerned with hurting your feelings, they may resist being candid," he offers.

Finding and working with a mentor means that you need to be willing to recognize that you need help and then ask for it. This isn't always easy to do. But if you can be honest with yourself about your needs and goals and do the work to cultivate your mentoring relationship, you will realize the benefits.

Having been in your position before, mentors are in a position to provide you with valuable insights as you face tough transition decisions. One active duty service member I spoke with was struggling with the decision of whether to re-up his duty service, join the Reserves, or exit the military. After spending time with a 30-year veteran who helped him his weigh options and discuss the choices, he was able to commit to further military service in a way that supported their family and met his larger career goals.

Mentors can also advise you on how to position yourself for the civilian job market. One veteran I know was medically retiring from the Army and didn't know how to talk about his injury and subsequent retirement to potential employers. He was nervous that his injury would make potential employers reluctant to hire him. After speaking with his mentor, he found the right language to explain what happened without sounding like a liability to their next employer.

Whether you seek assistance in writing your resume, practicing your elevator pitch, or preparing for your first interview, it's important to remember there are people who have gone through what you're going through now and are willing and available to help you. Finding and working with a mentor can be a great help as you navigate your military to civilian transition.

Mentee Success Stories

Are you still not convinced that mentoring is a good idea? Here are more examples of service members and veterans who found mentoring to be a key component of their transition:

- A veteran separating after eight years was focused on the path that aligned with her experience in the military but later chose to pursue her true passion after realizing that the dream was closer in reach than she had assumed.

- A veteran retiring after 28 years was focused on job titles that matched military titles but wasn't getting any calls. His mentor helped him open his perspective and consider jobs he would be more suited for.

- A veteran retiring after 20 years paid to have her resume done but wasn't getting calls. Her mentor edited her resume for free, and she received multiple job offers.

Finding Internships, Apprenticeships, and Fellowships

If the question "What do you want to do next?" truly has you stuck, internships, apprenticeships, or fellowships can offer you the opportunity to test the waters in a job before you fully commit to that career choice.

How Do Internships, Apprenticeships, and Fellowships Work?

An internship is an opportunity companies provide for a worker (intern) to receive on-the-job training at no or reduced pay. Internships can be for any period of time (a month, a year, whatever) and can be voluntary or mandated for a specific career path. Any type of company or industry can offer an internship.

There are many opportunities for internships: internships in the marketing department of a professional sports team, to project management internships with defense contracting companies, to internships in major animation studios in Hollywood.

Apprenticeships typically are internship-style arrangements but trade skills are involved. For instance, a welding apprenticeship might lead to a career as a professional welding journeyman. In this case, the apprenticeship is the entry to on-the-job training required to achieve certification and credentials.

Fellowships typically are seen as more graduate-level internships. Generally a fellow has more relevant skills, is able to join the company with some work experience, and can add value sooner than an intern might. Internships are ideal for someone with limited exposure and professional experience, whereas fellowships attract candidates seeking deeper professional understanding.

Internships as Job Interviews

Internships allow employers to assess talent by seeing how interns work, how their character and personality align with company culture and values, and whether they have leadership skills and potential. Many employers allow potential employees to intern before offering a full-time position. The internship then becomes like an extended job interview.

Companies offer paid and unpaid internships to give interested and qualified candidates an opportunity to see how the company works. Companies often post these opportunities on their websites and may post them to job boards and recruiting sites too. They list the requirements, opportunities for growth, and expectations at the outset, and seek interns who can meet their requirements and add value.

The SkillBridge Internship Program

SkillBridge is the internship and apprenticeship program offered by the Department of Defense. This program provides service members in good standing, with written approval by their unit commander, a chance to gain valuable civilian work experience and skills during their last 180 days of service.

Whether your goal is to earn your Project Management Professional certification, a Commercial Driver's License (CDL), or learn what it's like to work at a big civilian company, SkillBridge offers paths to get you there.

Participating in SkillBridge offers many service members these benefits:

1 You receive valuable training, certifications/credentialing or skill building at no cost. Although some SkillBridge programs do tap into GI Bill benefits, most do not. Imagine receiving your PMP certification, CDL, or Microsoft Certification before you exit the military.

2 You can do this work while still on active duty and earning a paycheck and medical benefits. You'll be working in the environment you may choose for a career, and although your employer isn't paying you, you aren't stressed about income.

3 An internship or apprenticeship can help you start acclimating to the transition sooner. By getting out of your military mindset on a daily basis, you can begin to imagine life after the uniform, helping you reintegrate when you finally do exit.

Corporate Fellowships Through Hiring Our Heroes

Offered by the US Chamber of Commerce Foundation, the Hiring Our Heroes Corporate Fellowship Program (CFP) offers transitioning service members professional training and hands-on experience in the civilian workforce with leading corporations. Participating companies seek the talents, skills, and experiences offered by transitioning service members. In return, they offer access to work style, culture, programs, and on-site opportunities within their businesses.

The CFP program runs three cohort programs of 12 weeks at select military installations and in host cities. Each cohort consists of 15 to 30 active duty service members and may also include veterans and military spouses. Once selected, candidates undergo on-the-job training at their host company, along with weekly educational sessions held in a classroom setting.

To be eligible for the CFP program, active duty candidates must be within 180 days from separation at the time of the 12-week program start. Candidates must have also earned either an associate's or bachelor's degree and have a specified period of leadership experience.

Leveraging Your Contacts and Relationships Gained on the Job

The people you meet during your internship, apprenticeship, or fellowship can become valuable and important parts of your career network going forward.

Before you depart from your internship, be sure to identify colleagues, peers, supervisors, cross-functional teammates, and industry contacts who could be resources to guide you upward and forward. Consider these tips for leveraging the relationship further.

- **Connect online.** This is an easy one. The contacts you'll meet in your internships will be familiar with who you are and how you work. Personalize the invitation to connect and add them to your online network to ensure you'll stay in touch after you leave.

- **Discuss mutual goals.** Be sure you learn what they need and want so you know how you can be of service to them. If they are building their career and decide to change industries, do you know someone who can help them? What common goals and interests do you share? Make sure your relationship is mutually beneficial.

- **Make sure they know what you want and are looking for.** Help your network help you by telling them what you are looking to do and where you need help. Now that you have shared an experience together and you have made a good impression, make it easy for them to help you.

- **Stay connected after you leave.** Civilians tend to change jobs and companies often, and while you might not see a benefit to your career based on where they work, that could change. Staying in touch ensures you don't have to reintroduce yourself to a valuable contact later on.

Internships and fellowships allow you to gain real-world experience and exposure to the work environment. Just as the employer is trying out the candidate, the intern or fellow gets to see how they like or don't like the work environment, company culture, job structure, and pace.

How to Be a Successful Fellow

As a fellow, you should be prepared to work and not just observe. Kevin Preston (USA, Ret.) hires many of the fellows his employer brings on. "We know they won't have all the experience and skills—they are military service members. But they are ready to add value and learn about our teams and processes. This makes it easy for management to envision them working long term in the team."

Preston provides the following advice for those looking to get the most out of their internship or fellowship.

1 Stay humble. You don't know everything about the company or the job. Understand that you're on someone else's turf and they know a lot about their business. It's OK to expose your weaknesses and vulnerabilities to advocates and mentors you'll meet on the job. Check in with them to be sure you're on track and solicit advice to help you succeed.

2 Be willing to work. Avoid becoming too selective or discriminating about the work you're asked to do. Try to experience all aspects of the job, company, and industry to see if it's what you'd want to do long term. In a fellowship, you'll be asked to rapidly adapt to your new environment. If you can't, you could fail.

3 Know when to be quiet. There's a time to speak up and a time to pull your boss aside and speak privately. Dan, who was hired through a fellowship program, recalls when he was given access to important (but confusing) information in a meeting. Instead of challenging what he was hearing at the time, he went to his company mentor afterward and ran the scenario by him. "Good thing you didn't speak up," his mentor offered. "As the new guy, it's important that you know your place and don't confront publicly until you have credibility."

Informational Interviews

Another way to learn about a company's culture, workstyle, and everyday environment is through an informational interview, which is the secret weapon of successful job seekers and empowered career professionals. Different from a job interview, an informational interview is an informal conversation with someone affiliated with the industry or the role the veteran is considering, like a current or former employee. This person can share helpful information that is not well known, such as details on company morale, promotions, salary, and the like. The purpose of the interview is for you to gain perspective, knowledge, or insight into a company or industry.

David Resilien (USMC, Ret.) encourages veterans to seek out informational interviews. While in the job hunt, in addition to conducting online research into roles and industries, Resilien recommends that you "always speak to a human, whenever you can. People will give you real insight and information into the job, the company, and the career field." Resilien suggests seeking informational interviews with people who are in the job you want or were there before. "They'll give you different perspectives from what you can garner online. It's important to hear about the job from someone in the job," he notes. "For example, if you learned about the Marine Corps by only watching television and movies, you'd have a very different view of what it's like to be a Marine. The commercials don't show us mopping or cleaning weapons. A Marine will tell you about that side of our job that the commercials don't show. They'll also tell you that, beyond boot camp, the Marine Corps is not someone yelling in your face 24/7. Speaking with a person familiar with the role will clear up misconceptions about the role."

Whom Should You Ask for an Informational Interview?

Professionals of all walks of life and at various stages in their careers might be willing to give you an informational interview.

To compile your target list of interviewees, think about what information you need to help you make your career decisions. When I started my company, I sought out informational interviews with anyone who'd started and grew a successful company. I wasn't concerned with industry—I spoke with everyone from a dry cleaner proprietor, to the owner of a retail store, to successful international consultants. I was more concerned with gathering insight and identifying patterns that made them successful.

If you choose to pursue education after your military service, you might speak to veterans who've pursued similar education paths or degrees, or even those who've attended the school you'll be attending. Look for individuals who will offer you information about the path forward and help you understand what to look out for as you navigate your career.

For those of you joining the corporate world after the military, you might identify professionals who are new to those careers, others who are farther along, and then those who've built successful and thriving careers. Each will give you unique and helpful perspectives.

Where Do You Find People Willing to Give You an Informational Interview?

Once you have identified the companies or industries you're interested in, look to your network to find people with the right experience who may be interested in sharing their insights with you. Other veterans will be inclined to help you because of a common history and service commitment. You can also use LinkedIn to find people who are keyword-tagged on the topics you wish to learn more about, who repeatedly show up on LinkedIn for their expertise in a field, or whom you are connected to already and have the skills, knowledge, or insight you're looking for.

You could also reach out to the people in your own network, who may know the people you want to know.

How Do You Ask Them for the Meeting?

In your outreach, be as specific as you can about what you need and why you seek to speak with them in particular. Whether you reach out by email, phone call, or text massage, start off with: "Hello, Mr. Smith. I read about your interesting career path from the Navy to tech startup and your path sounds fascinating. I am a weapons specialist, separating from the Marines in 180 days, and am curious about a career in information technology in the space industry, similar to yours. Would you be open to spending 15 minutes with me on the phone, discussing some critical questions I have, which will shape my career path forward? I am happy to schedule this call at a time that is convenient for you."

It's important to follow a few rules when you ask for an informational interview:

1 **Be clear about the ask.** What do you want to know, and why are they an ideal person to reveal the answers? If you are too vague, it may intimidate your subject, or they might fear you are too unfocused to have a productive call (and thereby a bad use of their time.)

2 **Specify a time contract for the call or meeting.** It is customary to request 15 minutes for a short call or 45 minutes for a more robust interview with someone you are more familiar with. This helps the interviewee set realistic calendar expectations.

3 **State that you aren't looking for a job with them.** It might sound odd to say it, but if the person you want to interview perceives this meeting as a bait-and-switch, that you really just want to use the meeting to sell yourself, they could turn you down. Even if the meeting turns toward your candidacy—by them, not you—it's important to state up front that you're looking for insight and information, not hitting them up for a job.

Dos and Don'ts for a Successful Informational Interview

- **Don't violate the time contract.** If you asked for a 15-minute meeting, let them know when you've approached the 13-minute mark. It's unfair to go past the time contract unless *they* want to pass it. The person you're interviewing may be inclined to keep chatting with you, and that's perfectly acceptable.

- **Do stay focused.** Have your thoughts and questions organized before you enter the meeting. Use the time well and you'll earn their trust and respect, making a positive impression.

- **Don't sell yourself.** Remember, you can't ask someone for their insight and information and then pitch them on you as a job applicant. If that happens organically, or if they ask you direct questions about your career path, then the rules change. Unless that happens, you must stick to the plan.

- **Do share something about yourself to build rapport and trust.** At the outset of the meeting, it is acceptable to provide some background on who you are and why you're having the conversation. This should resemble your elevator pitch as it leads into your first question. The focus on the interview is on them, not you.

- **Don't interrogate your interviewee.** Avoid shooting rapid-fire questions at your subject. You're not an attorney questioning a hostile witness in court; rather, you're looking to listen, learn, and leverage what they share with you into actionable steps to make choices and grow your career.

- **Do look for patterns.** When you ask similar questions to each of your interviewees, you'll be able to identify the similarities in their insight and feedback. I did this when I launched my own company—I always asked the same questions:

  a. What is one thing you did right when you launched your company?

  b. What is one thing that didn't work or that you wish you'd done differently?

  c. Given what I've shared about my venture, what advice would you have for me?

Following Up—A Critical Step

Following up after an informational interview is absolutely critical. If you do nothing else, circle back to your interviewee with appreciation and any deliverables you promised. If they offered to introduce you to a colleague or networking contact, pursue it. Even if you don't see the direct connection, trust their lead and follow up. If they offered input or suggestions for you to refine or look into, do it. At this point, your goal is to gather insight and information from which you'll make great career choices and decisions. Resist judging the information provided and accept it in the context offered: as guidance.

Let your interview subject know how their input or suggestion worked out. Did you meet with their contact? Did you pursue that advanced certificate? Did you consider their guidance? Someone who is willing to meet with you and share their input with you feels vested in the outcome of that insight. They want to know if their guidance helped you or if you need more. They truly care.

When you keep in touch with your informational interview subjects, you not only continue to build out your network, but you can tap into their expertise and feedback again, if needed. If you disappear after the meeting, they may feel unappreciated, unsatisfied, and reluctant to help you further.

Volunteering

Volunteering is yet another way to gain insight into what may be your next career. When you volunteer, you continue your commitment to service, increase your network of contacts, and broaden your skills and experiences. Volunteering allows you to serve. As a veteran, service to others or to a cause is likely an important component to your career goals. Volunteering is a way to deliver on that commitment, even if you aren't being compensated for it. When you serve, you help a population, cause, or constituency that needs what you can offer. The selflessness that comes from volunteer service strengthens your values, rewards you with gratitude, and helps others in the process.

Volunteering also helps you broaden your network. Surrounding yourself with like-minded individuals who serve a common cause helps you meet people from other backgrounds, experiences, skill sets, and communities who can add vibrancy and interest to your professional network as you build up your next career.

Last, volunteering can help you learn new skills. If you believe you want a career in public policy or advocacy work, try working for your local representative and see how things feel in that environment. Curious about starting a for-profit business serving pet owners? Volunteer at the local animal shelter and see what owners and their pets are like. Looking to run a tech startup one day? Volunteer in the fundraising efforts for a nonprofit to learn about the challenges and opportunities of development and fundraising.

Whether you volunteer five days a week for six months or just one day a month for a year, you will still gain the benefits from volunteer work. Focus less on the time restrictions and compromises you'll need to make to accommodate your volunteer work and more on the benefits and rewards gained.

In Closing

Getting out there means getting out of your comfort zone. As you choose a mentor, pursue an internship, apprenticeship, or fellowship, engage in informational interviews, or commit to volunteering, you will move past what's familiar and toward what might feel uncertain or unpredictable. Although it's important for you to research companies and jobs and build your profile on social media, don't forget to get out from behind the keyboard and connect in person.

Mentors, coaches, colleagues, and networking contacts can help support and guide you. Connecting with nonprofits focused on supporting veterans in transition will also provide you with resources and opportunities to grow your skills, experience, and confidence as you transition to your next career.

In the military, you learned to "embrace the suck." You learned that times will feel uncomfortable—or painful—and conditions less than optimal. When times suck, your job isn't to complain or retreat but rather to push forward, moving through the suck to the other side. Rely on this training to move out of your comfort zone and enlist some support.

Researching, Applying, and Interviewing for a Job

09

Progress is impossible without change, and those who cannot change their minds cannot change anything.

—George Bernard Shaw

The day you start applying for civilian jobs, you'll realize just how different this process will be from anything you've done before. You've likely never created a resume or had to sell yourself in a job interview. The changes coming now are going to feel fast and furious. My hope is that the steps I outline in this book will empower you to be confident and clear as you apply, interview for, and then choose a civilian job after the military.

Not all veterans find dream jobs immediately upon leaving the military. You might see the person on one side of you landing a job that starts immediately after they PCS for their last time. The person on the other side of you might profess such clear career direction that you believe the problem is you. You are somehow not figuring things out quickly enough; after all, they did.

In reality, the transition takes time. That service member who accepted a job and started the week after they separated may become quickly disillusioned and unhappy, leading to unemployment or a job change within months. According to an article titled "A Covert Job Problem for Military Veterans," almost half of all transitioning veterans leave their first civilian job within the first year, and almost 80 percent will leave before the end of their second year (www.kornferry.com/insights/articles/veterans-hiring-retention-memorial-day).

That person next to you who seems to have their future all planned out may be seeking the comfort of a concrete plan, rather than the discomfort of ambiguity. They may take years to find a job and career that feels good to them.

For planning purposes, I'd allow six months to find something that checks enough boxes to get you excited and avoids many or most of your career nonnegotiables. Keep in mind that there is only so much you can control about the hiring process. At many companies, the hiring process can easily take six to 12 weeks from application to job offer. Even though you can't control whether the company has an open position, you can position yourself to be attractive to the company and let it know when you're available to work.

There are numerous resources to guide job seekers through the hiring process. In this chapter, I focus on specifically on what you need to know as a transitioning service member.

As you begin the process of researching, applying for, and interviewing for positions, your mindset and attitude need to be sharp, positive, and focused. Try not to get frustrated, discouraged, and angry. Instead, cultivate a curious outlook, to be open to new opportunities and evaluate opportunities based on the criteria and filters we've set in this book. When you are confident, clear, and consistent, you'll make good choices for yourself, your family, and your career.

Researching Job Opportunities

Before you start applying for jobs, do your homework. You'll want to be sure you are seeking opportunities that align with your goals, values, and workstyle. This ensures you're making a clear and intentional move to build a thoughtful and focused career.

What to Research: The Industry

As you research career moves, consider the viability of the industry. Ideally, you'll want to target growth industries, such as those in science, technology, math, and engineering (STEM). A career in engineering or project logistics would leverage your technical training and your skills in project management, risk mitigation, and management—and your resourcefulness.

According to Cesare Wright, Ph.D., professor of engineering and a STEM specialist, "Veterans are an invaluable resource to private employers and defense contractors for careers in STEM. It is through their military training, real-world experience, and dedication to service that veterans bring unique skills that are directly transferrable to careers in science and technology."

If STEM isn't an area that interests you, consider other growth industries, such as finance, healthcare, design, or real estate. For any industry you choose, you'll want to learn all you can about trends, career options, market saturation, and what companies are in the lead position.

For industry research, consider news sites, academic sites that cover industry trends, and blogs that track global business developments. Each of these will highlight opportunities and weaknesses of various industries, in various geographies.

What to Research: The Company

As you research industries, certain companies might rise to the top of your list for their contribution, visibility, type of work, or leadership. For example, you may be attracted to companies because of your network's endorsement of their business, because you know people who work there, or because you've heard good things about their company. To learn what the company is, what it stands for, and whether you can envision a healthy career there, you'll want to answer strategic questions like these:

- **What is the company's mission and vision?** If this is stated on its website, can you find evidence of the company living this mission?

- **Whom do they serve?** Is the company clear about the population (communities, clients, and constituents) it cares about?

- **Who are the company's competitors?** What does the target company do better/worse than the competition?

- **What is the company's brand?** What values does it articulate and uphold in its employee experience, customer and community relations, and market interactions?

- **What is the company culture like?** Does it promote a team environment where employees are recognized and rewarded for new ideas, risk taking, and innovation?

- **Does the company have a strategic initiative to attract, hire, and retain military veterans?**

Next, look for tactical insights like these:

- **What challenges has the company endured?** How did it navigate the challenges? Do you admire or respect the way the company handled itself?

- **Is their business growing, stagnant or declining?** Are there opportunities to help them correct a declining business?

- **Are they hiring?** For what positions are they actively recruiting?

- **What do employees say about working there?** Do they speak of consistency of values, a supportive work environment, opportunities for advancement, and strong leadership?

- **Does the company have systems and programs to ensure success for veteran employees?**

Be strategic in your approach identifying companies. Chris McGraw, a US Army veteran and executive recruiter, says: "If you want to do supply chain or logistics work, look at companies who have distribution or fulfillment centers in your city." McGraw counsels veterans to "look past the obvious and toward the strategic. If you read online that a company in your area just won a big contract, and that will require hiring more staff in your area, jump ahead of the job posting and proactively reach out to someone in human resources or logistics. Start building the relationships before the jobs get posted."

Online research of individual companies starts with the company website. Peruse certain sections of the website, including the "About," "Careers," and "Leadership" or "Team" sections. In these areas, companies likely broadcast their values, mission, and successes to meeting that mission. You'll also get insight about company culture if companies promote their teams and ability to work well together.

McGraw also encourages job applicants to research the company's clients, successes, and challenges. "Get to know what they care about and where they're growing (or not) to further identify opportunities and show the company that you understand them and their business."

After the company website, review sites like GlassDoor, the company's LinkedIn page, posts on LinkedIn by employees, and industry blogs where current and former employees share their perspective of the company environment and culture. Keep in mind, however, that sometimes former employees who are unhappy that they are no longer employed might hold a grudge and can post misleading insights, to the displeasure of their past employer.

As you do your research, look for trends or patterns around work environment: Do people seem to like working there? Do they feel recognized and rewarded? Are there opportunities to contribute new ideas and voice opinions? Does the company seem to live the values it promotes?

Additionally, look for insights around the business and its viability. You might find the company is poised for acquisition or initial public offering, which will have implications for how the business is run and its future growth and your possible career opportunities inside the company. You might also learn that the company has leadership vulnerabilities and challenges, indicating that you might not be working with the same people a year from now.

Informational interviews can provide insight into the company culture and business. During your informational interviews, you could ask questions such as:

- What do you know now (about working for the company) that you wish you'd known then?
- Does the company promote from within?
- What do you know about the person or team I'm interviewing with?
- What do you like best about working for the company? Like least?

You can also gain insight into the company and its business through your personal networks. William Lu, a veteran of the US Navy, leveraged his network and mentors to help understand how to read published job descriptions, as companies use different language and narrative to describe similar jobs. His network also helped him understand company cultures and what he could expect in the interview process. "Companies like to personalize the application and interview process to their culture," Lu notes. "I didn't know this and relied on insight from my mentors to understand how variable these processes could be, and how to position myself correctly when applying, networking my way into the company, interviewing, and even when onboarding with my current employer."

Company Benefits to Research in Advance

Consider the type of work you'd enjoy and the compensation you'll need. For instance, if you're exiting the military without retirement benefits and have a family to support, you may find it hard to live on a straight commission-type income. In that case, you might look for a role in which your salary is *exempt*, meaning that you are on salary, you don't qualify for overtime pay, and you are expected to complete your work in the time period allotted. The most common exempt positions are executive, professional, administrative, and some business development roles. The benefit of an exempt position is that your paycheck is the same each week (or biweekly), so you can budget for the future.

Nonexempt employees are hourly and do qualify for overtime pay. According to the Fair Labor Standards Act, these workers must be paid one and a half times their hourly wage for work that exceeds 40 hours per week. Nonexempt employees can be paid minimum wage or another wage that is agreed to with employer and employee. Although the opportunity for overtime can help nonexempt employees earn more from time to time, it also means your paycheck may vary depending on the hours you work.

You should also research the company's time-off policy, which will be either PTO (paid time off) or FTO (flex time off). PTO creates a number or pool of days off each year that an employee can use for vacation, sick days, or personal days. Employees can use these days at their own discretion and should coordinate their time off with their managers in advance. FTO, in contrast, doesn't track the number of days off that an employee takes. It's thought of more as an "honor system" of days off. In other words, the employer trusts you won't abuse the privilege of taking as much time as you need and that you'll still get your work done.

The last work benefit to consider is where you'll work—at home, remotely, or in the office. For many employees, working in an office gives them structure, camaraderie, access to resources, and a sense of consistency. For others, remote or virtual work (working from home) allows them to pace themselves better, work more independently, and increase their effectiveness. Many companies allow for consistent or sporadic remote work from employees. If your lifestyle, schedule, or preference is to work remotely, consider companies that offer this option and flexibility.

Looking for Jobs

Civilian careers are not as clear or prescribed as a military career. It could happen that to get the experience you need for your dream job, you start by applying for positions outside of your specialty. For instance, if your dream is to work in international relations for a global consumer products company, you might start in the marketing, finance, or even human resources department to gain familiarity and exposure, ultimately moving into your ideal department once you have more experience.

You will likely begin to apply for jobs while you're still in uniform or on terminal leave. Some service members begin applying for jobs months before they've completed their military service and inform prospective employers that they won't be able to begin work until their commitment is finished.

Kevin Preston (USA, Ret.) advises service members to research the hiring practices of desired employers. "At some companies," Preston explains, "it can take months to get hired on. The paperwork, background checks, and multiple rounds of interviews all take time and can throw off a job applicant who needs to earn a paycheck more quickly. If you express desperateness or urgency during the interview process, you'll likely turn off the employer."

As long as you're forthcoming and truthful about your start date with your potential employer and the timing also works for the company, there is no harm to starting your applications early.

As you begin applying for positions, remember that you are looking for a healthy match between employer and employee, where you both thrive and grow. You aren't trying to convince someone to accept you or manipulate circumstances to your advantage. Beau Saltz, a specialist in recruiting and placing technology professionals in jobs in the Silicon Valley market, shares that "employers want to see mutual benefit with their hires. Regardless of the position, they want the candidate to feel it's as much of a 'win' as the employer does. Hiring is not a one-sided equation."

Just as employers have to manage misperceptions, biases, and myths in their hiring process, so will you as a job seeker. Resist telling yourself:

- "I was an executive officer in the Army. I'll only take an executive-level role in my civilian career."
- "I'll send 30 resumes out a week. Surely one of them will strike."
- "I'll let the recruiter figure out from my background if I'm a fit for the job."
- "If I list everything on my resume and application, they'll surely see how I could do this job."
- "I'll choose the first job I get offered to stop the worrying. I can always leave if I don't like it."

These myths set you up for disappointment and possible career struggles. Your past experience certainly helps employers understand where you might fit within their organizations, but a leadership role in the military does not automatically qualify you for a management role in a company. Similarly, applying for jobs should be done strategically and with precision, focusing your resume and cover letter to each position and showing the reader how and why you're a fit. It's not a numbers game. Although more applications could increase your ability to be interviewed, they likely won't increase the number of offers you receive.

Finally, avoid taking a job that isn't a good fit just because you want to stop looking. Choosing, accepting, and then leaving multiple jobs in a short time period makes you look like a hiring risk. You might get away with it once or twice, but listing too many jobs in a short time on your resume will make employers question your commitment, decision-making ability, and stability.

Reading and Understanding Job Descriptions

It would be wonderful if civilian job descriptions actually described the ideal candidate. Instead, job descriptions today provide a general idea of the kinds of skills the candidate needs and the types of experiences that might be relevant. Recruiters often refer to job descriptions as "advertisements," noting that particularly in job markets where there are more open positions than candidates, employers have to sell themselves to be desirable to attract key talent. Don't be thrown off if the posted job description looks like a marketing piece.

To successfully read a job description, consider these tips:

- There's a lot to the job that's not listed or outlined on the job description. When you read it, look for questions you'd want to ask and know more about to see if you're a good fit for the position.

- The description will read like a formula of skills the employer is seeking to recruit: Are the skills more technical, operational, organizational, or leadership related? Can you anticipate what other skills the employer will want to round out a viable candidate?

- Aside from translating your military skills (i.e., weapons maintenance) into civilian skills (i.e., mechanic), ask yourself what other skills you've developed that will be part of the formula the employer seeks. Did you manage budgets, procurement, or other people?

- Resist making a decision about the viability of your candidacy based on the job description alone. Although it will be important that you apply for jobs you *can* do, remember that there are skills, qualities, and talents the company seeks that won't be listed. If you check most of the boxes on the requirements, apply.

The job description does provide some hints at what the employer's ideal candidate will sound and work like. If job descriptions mention "passions," "vision," and "collaboration," employers will look for someone who speaks and acts that way. This is great insight for how you can position yourself, assuming you are passionate about creating collaborative environments where visions come to life.

Get Found by Thinking like a Recruiter

Recruiters can be a great help in your job search. Recruiters get paid for helping companies fill open positions, and they use tools like online job boards and LinkedIn to find people whose descriptions, profiles, and resumes contain the keywords for the positions for which they are recruiting. For this reason, having the right keywords on your profiles and resume is critical. If your profile or resume is a match, recruiters will reach out to find out if you are interested in pursuing the opportunity.

Recruiters also review the resumes of people who apply online directly or through relationships and networking. In these instances, recruiters are looking for two things. They are looking for candidates who did their research and know something about the company and the job. Most recruiters can detect when a candidate has sprayed their resume across the internet and isn't taking a thoughtful or focused approach. They are also looking for candidates who show some initiative. Although it's inappropriate to harass or pester a recruiter online, initiating contact, showing interest, and expressing excitement for an open position is a sign the candidate has thought about this particular job and company and sees a fit.

At the same time, you need to be careful not to cross boundaries. Recruiters avoid candidates who push too hard. Lauren Addy leads recruiting for a large financial services company. She shared a story about a candidate who reached out to her on LinkedIn to introduce himself and inform her that he had applied for a position online. But he took it too far when he tried to start a conversation with the company CEO and other senior leaders, using his message with Addy to imply there was a personal connection. This crosses a line. Boundaries—personal and professional—are to be respected at all times.

Going out of your way to approach a recruiter online and introduce yourself is acceptable in most cases. Asking to learn more about the company or the role is also generally accepted. Just be careful and respect stated policies. Some recruiters have a no-contact policy while others appreciate the initiative taken. Asking your network about this recruiter and their preference is a good first step to avoid a mistake.

Make Your Network Work for You

Justin Constantine (USMC, Ret.) is well known for his work advancing veteran hiring in civilian companies. He offers this advice to veterans:

> [N]etworking is not something that many veterans are typically comfortable with, but we have to embrace it. While we come from a background that frowns on bragging about our accomplishments, after you leave the military you have to be able to talk comfortably about what you can offer. Keep in mind that many people find jobs based purely on personal relationships and from letting others know what they are looking for through a variety of networking activities.
>
> When you met in person with your military career planners and explained to them where you wanted to go, what you wanted to do there, and why you wanted these goals, you were making a personal connection with someone and influencing their decision. As you progressed through the ranks, you had opportunities to talk with those senior to you about their recommendations for you or any assistance they could provide within their personal circles. This is all networking, and we are surrounded by it every day. The sooner you feel comfortable with the idea of networking, the more pokers you will have in the fire.

Constantine encourages networking in a job search beyond just how the other person can help you. "Talking with a wide group of friends and associates about what they are doing, what worked for them, programs they are aware of, or anything else that ties into your goals is not only a form of networking but often the best source of information for you," he explains.

Applying for Jobs

Applying Online

As you apply online for positions through a company's Careers page or an online job posting site like Monster.com, LinkedIn.com, or Indeed.com, your resume goes into an Applicant Tracking System (ATS). Bryan Dyer (USN) works in human resources and describes the

ATS this way: "It's an automated system that filters and evaluates applicants and their resumes against specific criteria the recruiter enters. Basically, an ATS is an algorithm that determines whether enough of the necessary criteria are met to put the resume into the 'for consideration' pile or not. The ATS helps the recruiter sift out resumes that are not a match for an open position and saves time reading hundreds of resumes."

In order for your resume to match an open position, you'll need to include focused and specific keywords that translate your military experience into civilian language so employers can understand what you've done and how it applies to what they're hiring for. If your resume lists your experience as an 03-11 Marine Rifleman but the position is for an operations manager, the ATS will reject your resume. As a staff sergeant, you may have managed people, directed operations, and been responsible for projects. Listing your experience as an operations manager (instead of rifleman) will push your information farther.

Additionally, job candidates should include keywords around soft skills, such as "team player," "strong communicator," "collaborative," and the like. Listing "leadership," "veteran," "recruiter," or other characteristics and qualities the role requires are helpful to recruiters and managers who'll see your resume.

Applying at Job Fairs

The recruiters you meet at a job fair will expect you to have a current version of your resume available, in print and/or electronically. In addition to bringing printed copies of your resume, consider bringing your resume with you on thumb drive (flash drive) to make it easy to upload electronically.

Applying Through Networking

Networking your way into the application process is by far the most impactful way to apply for a job. When someone you know personally walks your resume into the recruiter's office or emails them directly with an endorsement of your candidacy, the recruiter takes note. The recruiter may still need you to apply for the position through their ATS or other application formalities, but they now have your name, resume, and a glowing endorsement in hand. This often puts you at the top of their list for consideration.

Customize the Cover Letter and Resume

It is unrealistic to believe that a one-size-fits-all resume and cover letter will speak to each individual recruiter seeking a unique candidate for a specific job and team. Instead, consider relevant keywords and key phrases mentioned in the job description and repeat them where appropriate in your customized cover letter and resume. Use language that reflects the culture of the company in your cover letter. If the company's culture is family-like and supportive, you might highlight your passion for the industry, your desire to work collaboratively, and your ability to lead teams.

A Note About Business Writing

Throughout the application process, you will have opportunities to write to these targeted employers. At all times, consider these tips for effective business writing:

- **Spellcheck and proofread** all emails, letters, notecards, and social media direct messages.
- **Keep your message succinct and focused.** Avoid adding too much background and context to make your point.
- **Do not use texting-style abbreviations.** When we send text messages, it might be acceptable to say "thx" to a spouse for fetching the kids from school, but you should never type "thx" to an interviewer after a meeting.
- **Leave out emojis, gifs, clever fonts, and graphics.** Business writing is professional at all times.
- **Be sincere.** If you truly are excited about an opportunity, let them know. Showing sincerity and being genuine make you relatable and approachable.

Interviewing for the Job

A colleague of mine leads hiring for a large consumer products company. When she interviews qualified candidates, she always asks one specific question: "Why do you want *this* job?" She doesn't ask why they want to work for the company or want to work in that particular field. She wants to know what it is about this job, with this company, at this time that excites the candidate.

Chris Sanchez (USN, Ret.) shares: "Hiring managers will not connect the dots for you on recognizing the value you bring to the table. You need to control the narrative, considering that you'll be competing with others who have the direct experience the employer seeks while you don't. A personal brand is how you'll represent yourself and what you stand for—online and in person—and how hiring managers will remember you."

Today, employers utilize efficiencies and technology to interview candidates. Not all job interviews will be in person, one on one. You may find yourself interviewing by phone or video, and there may be several people in the room interviewing you in person.

Before you interview, research the person or people you'll be speaking or meeting with. Look at their LinkedIn profiles, ask your network about their interviewing style, and learn what their career history can tell you about how they'll interview and what they care about. You'll need this knowledge as you approach the interview.

Phone Interviews

Phone interviews are typically used for screening purposes. They give recruiters the opportunity to assess your professionalism and basic communication skills, clarify your technical skills and work experiences, and decide if further interviews are warranted.

For a phone interview, keep your physical environment clear of distractions so you can focus on your notes and your communications. The good news about phone interviews is that you can prepare notes on what you'll say and have them laid out in front of you. Even though the interviewer can't see you, you should take the opportunity to be well versed on your resume and ready to discuss all aspects of your qualifications for the job. Turn off any distractions—such as home phones, computer alerts—and ensure your family knows you are doing a job interview and shouldn't be interrupted. I once interviewed a candidate who was sitting in a crowded coffee shop. The background noise was distracting and disconcerting, and I questioned his judgment in choosing that location.

Video Interviews

Conducting interviews using video (Skype, Zoom, FaceTime, or another platform) is becoming increasingly popular with employers. There are many reasons employers are using video, including:

- The company wants remote employees to participate in the candidate's interview.

- It's less expensive than flying a candidate in to interview in person if the candidate is out of state.

- The interviewer can assess body language and professional appearance as part of their hiring criteria.

- Video allows for more rapport-building since there are visual cues in addition to verbal ones.

Before the video interview, download any software you'll need for the meeting. If you haven't done so already, create your online profile (i.e., Skype) so the recruiter can connect with you and download any software you'll need for the meeting. Do a practice run with a friend or colleague to ensure you sound good. Clean up the background of your room to remove distractions and clutter and dress as if you were interviewing in person. Wear the complete outfit. There are cases where the candidate wears only a suit jacket, shirt, and tie with shorts, not suit pants, and at some point needs to get up, revealing his attire to viewers. Besides, being dressed for an interview puts you in the right frame of mind for the meeting.

Most important, even though you can have some notes in front of you, you'll want to look at the camera during the video interview, not down at your papers. Resist looking at the computer screen or monitor, since the camera is typically higher. If it helps, place a sticker near the camera to remind you to focus there.

As you answer questions, pause and reflect for a second before jumping into a response. Show that you are thoughtfully considering the question and your response. Smile when appropriate. They are real people, after all.

Group or Panel Interviews

Group or panel interviews are where the candidate is interviewed by more than one person at a time, offering unique advantages to the employer. First, more than one person can experience the candidate's responses to the questions, and each interviewer will provide their own perspective on the candidate's qualifications and fit. Second, panel interviews help employers see how the candidate handles stress and their composure under unusual circumstances. Third, having more people interview the same candidate at the same time reduces the number of meetings, challenges of scheduling, and overall time it takes to evaluate each candidate.

As a candidate, navigating the group interview—where you're on one side of the table and the interviewers are sitting facing you—requires some different preparation. You'll need to research as many of the interviewers as possible. Understand their roles in the company and their experience levels, and try to assess their role in the decision-making process. Even with that research done, never assume you know someone's experience level or influence over your candidacy.

In the interview, you'll want to be as professional, poised, and focused as you would be in a one-on-one interview. The difference is that you'll get questions from multiple people. Be sure to make eye contact with everyone, not just the person who asked the question. Also avoid speaking to just the men in the room or the person who arranged the interview. Treat everyone with equal respect and attention.

It is fine to ask whether you answered their question if you are unsure. Asking "Did that answer your question?" is fine, as is "Would you like me to expand on that?" if you feel they aren't satisfied with your response.

Just as you do when you enter the room, at the conclusion of the interview, personally thank each interviewer. Offer a handshake and good eye contact. If you can, email each person afterward and/or send a follow-up thank-you written note to let them know you appreciated the interview and to reinforce your interest in the job and company.

How to Stand Out in a Job Interview

Whether it's a hot job market or not, candidates must always make a compelling case for themselves to get the attention of employers and to secure the best opportunities for their careers. As we discussed previously, your personal brand is about designing the perception you want others to have of you. You need to create and reinforce the reputation that will grow your career. The interview is a great place to let that unique value of yours shine.

When you are invited to interview, it means you have intrigued the employer in the application process such that they want to learn more about your skills and background and to evaluate if you are a good fit for the open position.

To stand out in a job interview, ask good questions. Resist asking the common interview questions found on the internet, and tailor your questions to the company, job, and interviewer. Instead of asking "What will the first 30, 60, 90 days in this job look like?," recruiting executive Addy suggests asking more specific questions related to the job, such as "From what I see about your onboarding process, and understanding that I will be participating in the company training program initially, what will my first few months look like? What will be expected of me in terms of results?" This shows the interviewer that you've done your homework and are interested in being successful.

You also want to express a desire to learn. Addy notes that candidates who stand out show an interest in growing their skills and experience and aren't impatient about promotions, raises, and job changes. "When someone acts like they already fit into our culture, we can more easily see them as a team member," she shares.

You want to display confidence but not arrogance. You want to communicate that you are confident you can do the job, are open to learning and growing, and you'll be easy for others to work with. Who wouldn't want to hire that person?

Last, you want to be consistent. What interviewers read in your application, resume, and cover letter should match what they see on your LinkedIn profile and should line up with who they meet in person. Strive for consistency in your positioning.

Mock Interviews: Practice Makes Perfect

Practice the interview with someone you trust. Run through how you'll handle questions, opportunities, and various hurdles. Ask for feedback on your message, body language, interaction skills, and the questions you asked of the interviewer. Be sure to refine your interviewing skills with each insight.

Translating Your Experience: Sell Your Value

The interviewer is looking to answer one question: Can this person do the job in the way we want? You need to ensure that you clearly communicate and present your experience, skills, and goals as valuable to the company.

In order to present your value, you need to show that hiring you will be of greater benefit to the company than the cost of your salary. When the benefit one derives is greater than the cost expended, there is perceived value. As you explain your technical skills, expertise, and training, relate them to the employer's needs and goals in value. As you describe your skills in leadership, problem solving, self-discipline, explain how they would add value to the company, the team, and the business's bottom line. Focus on how you can help solve problems for the employer. Be clear on what problems the company wrestles with, how you would solve those problems, and what value the company would extract from having those issues resolved.

Navigating Behavioral Interview Questions

Employers use behavioral interview questions to understand how the candidate thinks, reacts, and prioritizes. By asking candidates to describe certain past experiences or to imagine how they'd handle hypothetical scenarios, interviewers get a sense of a candidate's confidence, competence, and problem-solving skills. Your job, as the candidate, is to relate and translate your past experiences and competencies into a language they can relate to.

Here are some examples of behavioral interview questions:

- Tell me about your leadership skills.

- Describe your problem-solving abilities.

- Tell me about a time you had to work to solve an issue but had limited resources. How did you improvise?

- Tell me about a time you had to discipline a subordinate. What was the outcome and how did you approach it?

- Tell me about a time when you faced a roadblock in your ability to succeed on a project. What did you do?

- Describe a time when you had to innovate or create a new approach to a situation.

- How do you manage stress?

- Tell me about a time when you worked for someone you didn't respect.

- Tell me about a time when your plan fell short, when you didn't achieve your goals.

Respond with examples, stories, and scenarios that paint a picture of what you did in the past and indicate how you'll respond to a similar situation in the future.

Responding Using the STAR Method

To respond to a behavioral interview question or any interview question where this applies, use the "STAR" approach: Describe the Situation, Task, Action and Result.

Situation refers to what was happening. What events set up the situation? What was your role in the situation? Paint a picture of "what was" to frame what you did.

Task speaks to what you were trying to accomplish. What was the goal of the situation?

Action refers to what you did and the steps you took to achieve the goals of the task. As a veteran, your inclination will be to say "we," as in "We did...," but it's important that you speak in first person whenever possible. The listener wants to hear what *you* did to achieve the outcome.

Result is what happened. What outcomes did you produce? What result came from your efforts, and what did you learn from the experience? Whenever possible, quantify your results. If you can, show a percentage increase in cost savings or a number of staff members retained.

What Interview Questions Should You Ask?

Always ask questions of the interviewer. List your questions on a sheet of paper for reference and bring it to the interview in a notebook or portfolio. As the interviewer answers some of your questions during the natural flow of the interview, mark them off on your sheet. When the interviewer asks you, "What questions do you have for me?," be ready to reply.

In initial interviews, ask questions about the job and company culture. Avoid questions about promotions and salary progression. Some good questions to ask in an interview include:

- **What attracted you or has kept you at the company?** This question makes interviewers reflect on why they like to work at the company and will showcase various aspects of the employee experience they value.

- **Can you clarify this aspect of the job for me?** Ask about a specific responsibility or duty that you're unsure or unclear on.

- **Where do you see this job's department going in the next three years?** A question about growth for the team shows you care about others as much as your own career path.

- **Is there anything we've talked about or that you've seen in my background that you'd like me to clarify or expand on?** Offer an opportunity to add additional context and examples to your experience in case the interviewer forgets to.

Presenting yourself as a desirable candidate doesn't mean selling yourself into the job or gaming the system to get the offer. You want to attract offers that you'd strongly consider. In order to evaluate offers, you need to clarify the role to see if it is something you can picture yourself doing. Consider the nonnegotiables you discussed with your family when you plotted your career plan. Do you have questions around how the job might impact those boundaries? The interview is where you'll clarify them, not at the offer acceptance phase.

Ending the Interview: Next Steps

For a sales or business development role, you'd certainly want to nail the close of the interview. The interviewer will be evaluating your sales skills, and asking for the sale is a critical part. For positions where you feel less inclined to directly ask for the job, inquire about next steps. If it isn't clear to you, ask what to expect next in terms of process. In a professional manner, ask when you will hear back and what the next step in the interview process is and the time frame for checking references. Be sure you leave the interview with an understanding of what happens next to reduce anxiety, manage your own expectations, and fulfill any expectations the interviewer has of you.

Following Up on the Job Interview

It is acceptable to follow up on an interview if you haven't been told otherwise. The recruiter might tell you that they are reviewing applications and interviews and will contact approved candidates in a month. Don't pester the recruiter during that month. Follow up and thank them for the interview, reiterate your interest in the position and willingness to provide any additional information they need, and then stand down. If you interrupt the recruiter too often inquiring about your status, you'll be perceived as a nuisance.

If you don't hear back in the time frame they outlined, it is acceptable to inquire about your application status. If they are not moving forward with you, it is also acceptable to ask for any feedback or input about where you could have done more or where you weren't a fit. Many recruiters are too busy to offer feedback to each candidate, but if you are fortunate to find one who is willing, their insights can be extremely helpful and useful.

Interviewing Dos and Don'ts

- **Do practice interviewing with friends, colleagues, and even at jobs you aren't sure about.** You don't want to have your first real interview at your dream job where you may be still be rough. Practicing helps you work out the kinks.

- **Run through various responses to behavioral interview questions.** When you can, consider responses using the STAR method.

- **Do your research in advance of the interview.** Be informed. Don't start an interview with questions like "What do you guys do here?"

- **Don't assume you've got the job because you did well on the interview.** Some companies require multiple interviews before they make an offer.

- **Don't let your guard down in an interview.** Although you'll want to be relatable and approachable, being too casual or relaxed can put off interviewers. A job interview is a formal situation. Show interviewers respect by being professional.

- **Don't use too many military acronyms.** This only confuses interviewers if they are not former military or do not have a deep knowledge of military lingo.

- **Don't curse or make jokes that could be offensive.** When in doubt, keep the joke or questionable comment to yourself.

In Closing

Securing your first post-military job requires thoughtfulness and focus. It's not about getting "any" job. You want to choose a job that lays a foundation for your career path, that leverages your talents, passions, skills, and experiences in a way you find meaningful and rewarding.

Start with the research and learn all you can about the industry, companies, and people you'll approach. Apply for positions that intrigue you and where your skills align enough to initiate the conversation. As you move through the interview process, evaluate the systems, culture, and vision of the company to further assess alignment with your broader goals and objectives.

Choosing and Beginning Your Career, Education, and Business Venture

10

You are now a civilian, no longer in uniform. Even if you've spent several weeks on terminal leave or in civilian environments as part of your military duty, leaving the military will feel different. As Chris Sanchez (USN, Ret.) shares, "It's different on the outside compared to the culture you are accustomed to in the Department of Defense. Some aspects are worse, some are better. Now is the time to be in 'sponge mode,' taking in as much as you can learn about your new life and position."

Choosing a job seems like the easy part, right? You just pick the first one offered or the one with the highest salary. Not so fast. Your job choices should fit into your overall career strategy. Just because a position has a great title or salary doesn't mean it's right for you.

How to Choose a Job

One of the hardest things you'll do in your civilian career is pass up an otherwise great opportunity because it's not great for *you*. Professionals and entrepreneurs often reflect that the times they said "no" were as impactful as the times they said "yes." A job that appears exciting but doesn't align with your values or vision for your future could negatively impact your career.

To be ideal, the job you consider should meet your minimum criteria. It satisfies your requirements around work style, compensation, and growth potential, and reveals a confluence of your strengths and goals. If it meets these criteria and you like the company and people, it may even be worth taking a slightly lower starting salary or a less impressive job title to get going.

Should You Negotiate the Offer?

Employers will offer you the job after they have completed their due diligence, checked your references, conducted a few rounds of interviews, and evaluated your abilities and skills.

The job offer reflects the perceived value of the work you will do for the company in consideration of market rates and budget for the position. Although the hiring manager may be empathetic to your situation, your compensation is not based on your personal needs or expenses. Your salary, benefits, and perquisites (bonuses, stock options, car expense reimbursements, etc.) reflect the value of the work you will do for the company as well as the experience and skills you need in order to perform well in that position.

As soon as you receive an offer package, whether in person or by email/mail or phone, you should immediately thank the sender by return email or during the phone conversation. Let them know that you appreciate the offer and will get back to them shortly. In most cases, it's not advised to accept a job offer on the spot. Employers expect that you'll want to review the details of the offer by yourself or with your family, clarify any outstanding questions, and perhaps negotiate the offer further.

If you don't know how or what to negotiate in a job offer, you're not alone. "Salary negotiation is one of those things that most people are lousy at, not just veterans," notes Byron Chen, Marine veteran and author of the book *Barracks to Boardrooms: Negotiating Your Salary After Serving in the Military*. Chen notes that studies show nearly half of employees never negotiate their salaries, yet most hiring managers are willing to negotiate on initial offers and many are flexible on other perks and benefits, if not the base salary. Chen explains, "Most people struggle with overcoming the doubt they have that they *can* and *should* negotiate." They tell themselves that the employer will treat them fairly, they fear they will be rejected if they ask for an increase, and they worry about being seen as greedy if they try to negotiate past the initial offer.

Chen continues:

> I remember accepting my first job offer after leaving the military. Months of refining my resume, networking, and interviewing finally paid off—I was ecstatic! And with this offer, I wondered to myself if I should negotiate it. I reached out to my network of friends and family for advice. After all, they had guided me so well through my transition. They told me mostly the same thing. No, don't negotiate, be happy that you got the job. So, I didn't. About a year later, I was doing some research on the job market and learned that I was earning well below the industry average. I had the same level of experience and education as my peers, so why the disparity in compensation? I went back to ask my friends and family. What I found out was that almost none of them had ever negotiated their salaries before.

Not negotiating your salary ends up being a costly mistake, Chen notes. It's important to consider the long-term effects. Your raises and bonuses are calculated from your salary, and any future compensation packages at new jobs are largely based on what you made previously. Over your career, this could add up to tens of thousands of dollars in more earnings if you negotiate successfully.

How to Negotiate Salary, Terms, and Compensation

When negotiating compensation, it's important to recognize that there may be a better opportunity ahead if you start a step backward. In other words, if you enter a company in a more junior position but you know the company promotes from within, you might grow faster than if you hold out for a more senior initial opportunity.

Chen advises every job applicant to negotiate their first job offer. His tips for negotiating a job offer include these:

1 **Do your homework.** Know the standard industry salary for the position you've been offered. Sites like Payscale.com, Salary.com,

LinkedIn.com, Glassdoor.com, and Visadoor.com publish salary information from various industries and positions. Candidates can also speak to people in the industry to learn more about expected compensation. Use this information to set your salary expectations and career growth goals.

2 **Think beyond just salary.** If the position you're being offered has a salary cap or the employer can't justify a higher salary because of your lack of skills or transferrable experience, look at other compensation perks. Extra vacation days, an expense account, or professional development funds could provide value that you can credit toward your overall compensation.

3 **Ask.** Most people think they have to be expert negotiators or risk ruining their careers. Be sure you approach any negotiation with respect and your research in hand. Today, employers expect a certain amount of negotiation so the initial offer may be lower than they are willing to pay. Be professional and courteous in your dealings, and the employer will treat you the same.

Before You Accept

Once you have a job offer and have negotiated a compensation package, make sure you have answers to all of your questions. Do you understand what will be expected of you in the first few months or years? Are you clear about chain of command and where to go if you have additional questions? Do you understand how paychecks are distributed—is it monthly or bimonthly? Is your family comfortable with the offer? If the job involves extensive travel, will you have your family's support to do so?

Make sure you are honest with yourself about why this is an attractive offer to you. This job should be a step to your new career, not simply a way to check a box on your transition path.

As mentioned earlier, sometimes you'll accept a position that isn't ideal in the short term but has longer-range potential. Lisa Rosser (USA, Ret.) shares how her first civilian job out of the Army was not what she'd hoped for: "I was interviewing with a well-known global consulting firm when I left the military. They liked that I'd managed more than 120 soldiers, with my five direct reports all being senior enlisted personnel. In the Army, I had experience in high-stress scenarios, and I'd built a reputation as a commanding, forward-thinking individual. When the job offer came in, however, the position I was offered was managing five recent college graduates, and I felt it was quite junior to what I'd done in the military. At first this set me back. I wondered if I'd be hurting my career to accept something of a lower 'rank' and status than I'd just left in the military."

Rosser learned that the opportunity actually presented great career potential. "In the military we know that sometimes you have to slow down to speed up," she notes. "I was now being asked to manage a group of inexperienced individuals, which I initially found disappointing. Instead, over time I realized that while I'd been responsible for 120 soldiers in the Army, I'd actually managed five senior enlisted personnel who handled the 115 others. These were the officers who managed the privates, not me." In essence, she had very different management skills.

Rosser thrived in the role and grew quickly in her career. She found that learning something new is always momentum forward and that sometimes you need to reframe things in order to see the value.

Before you accept the offer, get comfortable with your vision for your career and how a position that might feel like a step backward, or lateral, could propel you forward faster.

Turning Down a Job Offer

Unfortunately, not every job is ideal for you. Sometimes you must turn down a great job offer for personal reasons or because it doesn't line up with your greater career goals. A less desirable job offer might feel easier to reject but even a good offer should be rejected with care.

Rejecting a job offer should never be about retaliation or anger. One day you may apply for another job with this company or may work for or with them in another capacity. You want to conduct yourself professionally and be respectful.

Begin by thanking them for their consideration and the offer, acknowledge that you gave the offer much thought, and tell them that you respectfully decline the offer. You do not need to provide a detailed reason for rejecting the offer unless you choose to. Avoid being hurtful ("You insulted me with that salary") or retaliatory ("One day you'll regret not giving me the higher title"). Instead, you could explain it this way: "Thank you for the consideration and offer to join your company. After careful consideration, I've decided to pursue an opportunity that more closely aligns with my professional goals and aspirations. I look forward to crossing paths again in the future."

Accepting a Job Offer

If you are convinced this is a good move, accept the job verbally and follow up with an email or letter of acceptance. Most employers will send you a written offer confirming all the details of the arrangement. Review this and sign documentation as required.

You will also be asked to submit a W-4 (for an employment opportunity) or W-9 (for an independent contractor role) and to schedule logistics for your employment. You'll pick a start date, discuss any training or onboarding programs you'll need to participate in, and go over logistics for relocation if that's part of the offer.

Onboarding

What Is Onboarding?

Onboarding is an employer's way of welcoming you to the company and familiarizing you with its rules, systems, and policies. There are formal and informal aspects to any onboarding process, and you may onboard on your own (as a one-off hire) or as part of a group or cohort of hires.

The onboarding process typically covers topics including these:

- **Description of company culture, mission, vision, and purpose.** The company's brand and values are integral to team building, market positioning, employee experience, and customer relations, so it's crucial that all employees understand what the company stands for and holds dear.

- **Rules around compliance, what's acceptable behavior from employees, and legal and regulatory policies that are in place.** This part of the onboarding process ensures all employees understand and agree to adhere to the formal rules of the company. Rules may include policies around sexual harassment, submission of expense reports, what qualifies for termination, and so on. In some cases, companies will include rules around dress code, appropriate employee relationships, and the process for filing grievances.

- **What you can expect.** Companies that paint realistic pictures of what it takes to be successful at their company and set expectations around reward systems, team building, leadership potential, and promotability report increases in retention and employee satisfaction. The belief is that when employees understand what to expect on the job, they are more committed to the company and the work.

Some questions to ask during your onboarding:

- **Does the company typically promote from within?** Companies that routinely seek managers and senior leaders from outside the company might be less inclined to promote someone from within the organization. Some companies believe that a fresh perspective and intelligence from a competitor's business is more valuable than the legacy institutional knowledge a current employee brings to senior leadership.

- **Are there initiatives that could benefit me as a veteran?** Perhaps the company is pushing to promote more military veterans into leadership roles. In this case, focus on accentuating your experiences in the military and reveal your skills and abilities by excelling in your current role.

- **How have others successfully grown their careers here?** Is the path to success at this company relationship based? Is it about knowing the right people and having them publicly promote your value? Is keeping a lower profile more positively rewarded in the company?

- **Do I have the credentials and education needed for growth?** And, if not, can the company help me attain them? Some companies recognize advanced education as a prerequisite for advancement. No matter how great employees are, they don't get into management without a master's degree, for example. Many companies offer training programs or subsidies for employees to advance their education and skills.

Onboarding can be conducted:

- **Offsite.** In this case, new hires are sent to a training program where they gather with other new hires from across the country or region. This can be for a couple of days or weeks, depending on the job and the company. Some companies train new hires on sales processes, technical systems, and other processes with a hands-on experience before sending them back to their location to start work.

- **On the job.** The expectation here is that you'll learn about the company culture by working within it. You'll learn what the dress code is by asking around or watching how others dress. You'll understand what it takes to be promoted by applying for advancement and being chosen or passed over. These real-world experiences work well for some candidates who prefer to learn in real time, but for others it can feel ambiguous and arbitrary, requiring them to seek out their own answers.

- **Online.** It's not uncommon for a company to instruct new hires to watch a series of onboarding videos to acquaint them on processes, procedures, and systems they'll be working with. Typically, there's an expectation that the new hire will complete these videos and any accompanying paperwork by a specific time.

Company Culture

Companies pride themselves on having cultures that support the business mission and attract and retain key employees. The company culture may be clearly articulated on the website or may be an understood way of working. Either way, your job in the first six months is to learn the culture and develop ways to work within the culture's standards.

Company Culture and Unwritten Rules

William Lu (USN) remembers the first time he went to a team meeting with his first employer. "I arrived early," he said, "because in the military early is on time and on time is late." As the rest of the team meandered into the meeting, Lu says, they glared at him and made snide comments about his trying to gain favor with the boss by being first on the scene. This type of misunderstanding is very common in your first few months on the job. As you learn about company work styles, culture, and the unwritten rules and codes of conduct, you'll find it easier to fit in, make friends, build credibility, and grow in your role.

One of the best ways to assess and understand the company culture and norms is by observing. What do others do? Are there systems and processes that are unwritten but widely accepted and adopted? Are these systems sanctioned by senior leadership or merely tolerated? For example, if your colleagues are repeatedly late to meetings your boss has begun, this may be tolerated because your boss accepts their behavior, even though he may privately consider it to be rude. Your boss might appreciate your timeliness as a sign of respect.

You could also just ask. You might ask your boss about rules and systems that aren't documented or even internalized, but clarifying what you see and what's expected is important. There also may be unwritten rules regarding the dress code and expectations around conduct away from the office and behavior on social media. Understand that unlike in the military, where standards are documented and understood, some of these systems are more nuanced and accepted rather than formalized in the civilian workplace.

Other veterans at the company can provide guidance and a heads-up on many of the unwritten rules you'll all operate within. Resist the urge to refute or dismiss the rules because they aren't what you're used to. Instead, understand that the fluidity of the company culture often means going with the flow.

Understanding Your Career Path at the Company

Much of what you experience in your new job is unwritten and may feel arbitrary. Why does one person get promoted but another is repeatedly passed up? Why are some employees given latitude in their work style while others are held to rigorous standards? How is it that some teams thrive and others barely survive?

Although your boss may give you an idea or outline of what makes "most" people successful at the company, the path to success or failure is not always clearly noted. It may be unclear at first, but you will figure it out as you observe, ask questions, and grow more comfortable in the culture.

Similarly, if you have a goal of management or senior leadership, it will be your responsibility to seek out mentorship and resources to position you for those roles. You'll identify the relationships, results, successes, and rewards that position someone like you to be successful in achieving the goals you set. No standardized, published diagrams will be provided to you like a roadmap.

Avoiding Job-Ending Mistakes

Your focus will be on doing everything right, but some inadvertent mistakes you can make may prove to be job-ending. Pay attention to:

- **Work style.** You're likely accustomed to arriving early and running meetings with a focused, directed, and tactical style. This expectation may not play well in the more collaborative and experiential work style of most civilian businesses. Resist the temptation to adhere to things as you did them in the military. You aren't right and your new coworkers aren't wrong. This new environment requires that you adapt to the standards and norms the company works within.

- **Social media.** Although your Facebook and LinkedIn accounts are yours, what you post online can have direct consequences on the job. If you inadvertently shared confidential or proprietary information or news or you acted in an offensive manner online, your employer can end your employment. Companies have very low tolerance for online behaviors that are outside culturally and socially acceptable boundaries.

- **Picking the wrong friends.** Be friendly to everyone, but wait to make close friends until you have a sense of who could potentially harm your reputation. The risk of picking the wrong friends is that you get branded along with them, even if you later realize they were not healthy for your career.

- **Harassment.** Bullying, harassment, taunting, and any behavior that may be tolerated in other environments are not tolerated in civilian companies. Liabilities and lawsuits make headlines. Public relations nightmares are risky for the company's image and brand. Companies have zero tolerance for employees who mistreat other employees. Get clear on where those boundaries are drawn to avoid a costly mistake.

- **Getting typecast.** If your natural style is to be more reserved and conservative in sharing your insights or ideas, consider what the team and your boss value. If they value contribution, risk-taking ideas, and collaboration, then holding back can jeopardize your role on the team. Likewise, you may want to avoid constantly speaking up and stopping the flow of a meeting or discussion. Observe for yourself what is acceptable and avoid being typecast as either the quiet shy mouse or the class clown.

Being Your Best Every Day

Whether you chose this first job because it represented everything you dreamed of or because it put you on the path to your career, make a commitment each day to be the best employee, leader, or team member that you can be. Go to work each day with a fresh perspective, and add value and grow. No one is forcing you to be at work, and employers can decide not to invite you back if you have a poor attitude.

If you later decide you chose wrong and need to make a change, do so elegantly and confidently without tarnishing your reputation. For now, while you are working, commit to living as the best version of yourself every day.

If you get the offer, negotiate and consider what you find acceptable, ensuring your professional boundaries and nonnegotiables are intact. If you have to reject the offer, do so with decorum and professionalism.

Beginning Life as a Student Veteran

Whether you are returning to school to complete an associate's degree or a bachelor's degree, or to pursue a master's or specialized degree, you will find yourself learning alongside students younger than you and with very different life experiences. As a student veteran, you'll likely be older than other students on campus. As a "nontraditional" student, you may find it challenging to fit in with groups or cliques and that you are less able to relate to the experiences of classmates. Rest assured, you can change this.

As a student veteran, consider:

- **Connecting with other veterans.** Most colleges and universities have a student veteran center and programs to support students who served in the military. Consider pursuing a leadership role in the Student Veterans of America chapter at your school, which can offer you great networking opportunities and exposure to various national programs and development trainings.

- **Getting a checklist of requirements to become a student.** Talk to a counselor in your veterans' center who'll provide you with a checklist to walk through before becoming a viable student. Your counselor can show you how to gather your DD214, shot records, medical history, academic transcripts, and other requirements to become a student.

- **Speaking to academic advisors in your degree program.** Be sure to ask about the program requirements, opportunities, and whether any of the programs permit obtaining licenses while in school, if this is important to you.

- **Seeking opportunities to build your personal brand and marketing yourself.** You might think you're a full-time student, but employers often recruit students before graduation. Look for high-visibility leadership opportunities to grow your network or build your name. Positioning yourself well as a student can help you position yourself well as a job seeker.

- **Finding a degree program that leads to a viable career.** Although it might be fun to study botany or midcentury architecture, will you have job offers when you graduate? Your mission as a student veteran is to graduate and then have a meaningful career. When evaluating degree programs, ask yourself: Can I add value with this degree and continue to serve in the ways I want? Can I support myself and my family with a job after graduation and into my future?

Dos and Don'ts for Student Veterans

Certainly, find places to connect with others. Join study groups to interact with other students and share insights and information. If you find these groups challenging, seek out study groups arranged thorough your veteran center, where you'll be alongside others with a military background. Look for seminars, lectures, and career development programs that put you in the room with others interested in the same topic. Doing this helps build collaboration and camaraderie and can launch friendships. Get yourself out there; resist hiding out in your apartment or the library when not in class.

This next suggestion may be a hard one. When you find yourself interacting with nonveteran students, avoid talking nonstop about your military experience or posing as superior to your classmates. Your experience prior to school is likely filled with significantly more challenge and diverse experience than that of students who just graduated high school and haven't ventured out into the world yet, but that doesn't mean your experience is better and theirs is worse. Your paths to college are just different. When you recognize and embrace the differences you all bring to the classroom, you open up the possibilities for communication and learning.

Consider internships and apprenticeships to help you learn firsthand what it's like to work in the companies you might want to pursue after graduation. An internship with a desirable employer can lead to a full-time job offer if you impress the company with your talents.

Getting involved in clubs and sports helps demonstrate your team skills and leadership abilities to potential employers. You'll also make friends and expand your circles of influence to teammates, coaches, professors, and student leaders. All of these new connections can be tremendous professional resources after graduation.

When things seem tough, remind yourself that transitions take time. Lisa Rosser (USA, Ret.) reminds veterans, "You didn't become a service member overnight. You had to learn the system and then things fell into place. You also had a drill sergeant screaming at you. No one is yelling at you now."

Beginning Life as a New Entrepreneur

There is no success formula for starting a technology company, running a consulting firm, building a new widget, or launching a business initiative. There are, however, some entrepreneurial best practices that you can adopt to help get your idea and company off the ground.

Start with a Business Plan

If you haven't done so yet, outline your business idea and vision, initial startup needs, and a description of the market for your product or service. A solid business plan is critical when starting a new venture, and numerous templates and resources are available to help you craft yours.

Decide how you will fund your new business. Do you have the money to start it yourself? Will you approach family and friends for a round of cash infusion? Will you seek a bank loan? Programs through the Small Business Administration in partnership with the US Department of Veterans Affairs offer great counseling and incentive packages to veteran entrepreneurs, particularly for veterans who qualify for disadvantaged veteran status.

Matthew Kuta (USAF, Ret.) grew his career from an F-15E fighter pilot in the United States Air Force to private equity investor on Wall Street before he launched his own venture. He shares the following advice for veterans pursuing entrepreneurship, especially right out of the military.

- **Be clear about what you're moving toward.** For instance, if your role in the military was focused more on managing people than doing the technical work, you might underestimate the amount of hands-on work required to craft and launch a business. If your experience didn't offer you the specific skills for the business you want to launch, consider working in the field, getting additional education, or finding other ways to build your knowledge base and skills.

- **Learn how to think like a businessperson.** The US Department of Defense is the largest nonprofit in the world, notes Kuta, and nonprofits don't think or operate like businesses do. Before you can craft a business plan, approach investors, or take your idea to market, you need to understand how business works. As a business owner, you'll need to know the difference between revenue and profit, how the points on a financial statements interconnect, and what problems you can anticipate as you grow. Many veteran entrepreneurs find it makes sense to spend the first few months and even years pursuing programs through the Small Business Administration, studying for an executive MBA, or working directly in industry.

- **Learn how to sell yourself, your vision, and your team.** Upon leaving the military, you're still in the culture of warrior ethos and service before self. "It's unnatural for veterans to talk themselves up," notes Kuta. But now, as an entrepreneur, you'll have to sell your personal brand, your business, and the partners and employees you've engaged. For many veterans, this feels slimy.

  Investors, business partners, allies, and even employees want to invest in you. They want to attach themselves to someone who will be successful, who will grow the vision to life, and who will partner and work with them. Learn how to tell your story in a way that is compelling and meaningful.

- **Focus on short-term gains and don't lose sight of the long-term vision.** There will be great wins (investments, deals closed, strategic hires, etc.) and losses (lost investments, lost deals, loss of key talent, etc.). Your ability to endure the ups and downs requires an understanding of the process and the business landscape as well as an ability to learn everything you don't know about starting and growing a business.

Taking Care of *You*

In any transition, you need to take care of yourself. This may feel awkward and different because your time in the military was always about caring for others.

It's important to learn techniques to help you manage the stress, frustration, and anxiety that will surface during this time. Some good techniques to follow include these:

- **Deep breathing.** When we're stressed, our breathing becomes quick and shallow. If you feel yourself getting stressed, focus on taking deep breaths and let the air travel through your lungs and down to your belly button. Doing this might feel strange, but it helps to increase lung capacity, slow your heart rate, and give you the mental clarity to manage stress.

- **Exercise.** Get into a regular exercise habit to keep your energy level high and your stress in check. If you are a runner, like to lift weights, or enjoy power cycling, this is a great time to actively pursue these hobbies. Find a form of exercise that feels good to you and gets your heart rate up so you can positively channel the energy you might otherwise spend stressing and fretting.

- **Socialize.** Being around other people helps to take our minds off our own problems and helps us to think about others. Find groups of people who lift your spirits, share similar interests and passions, and have healthy ways to gather and be together.

- **Moderate indulgences.** Without realizing it, many people self-medicate and attempt to manage stress with alcohol, cigarettes, marijuana, overeating, and other vices. These are temporary soothing mechanisms that, when not moderated, can lead to serious physical and mental health struggles.

- **Talk.** Share your concerns, frustrations, anxiety, sadness, and excitement with others. In some cases, it's warranted to talk to a mental health provider; in others, you can open up to your spouse, friends, or parents. Let those people around you know what you're feeling and bring them into your transition process.

- **Write.** I advise my clients going through stressful situations and transitions to write. Write down every feeling, emotion, fear, excitement, and suspicion. It's best if you can hand-write your feelings, as studies show that putting pen to paper affords a greater emotional release and more mental healing than typing our thoughts into a computer or tablet. Either way, if you just start writing, you'll see the value in letting the feelings come from your head and heart and into type.

- **Relax.** Being physically healthy requires some down time, so find time to relax and rejuvenate. This is an important part of being able to move forward and care for yourself and others.

Managing Expectations

Timelines vary when transitioning to a new career. If you'll be starting your own company, this can mean months of meetings with potential investors, business partners, employees, and more. If you'll be starting school, there may be a gap between the day you leave the military and when the next semester begins. For those of you in a job search, there is no definitive timeline for getting a job. It can happen fast or take months to navigate the hiring process.

"One of the most frustrating parts of my transition," explained a young female veteran who left the Coast Guard after a ten-year commitment, "was being asked repeatedly by my family when I'd have a job lined up."

As hard as it might be, try to assume good intentions from those around you who are curious (and maybe anxious themselves) about your ability to land on your feet after the military. Unless you have direct knowledge that they are inquiring to undermine your success, assume good intent on their part and respond by helping to manage their expectations.

Managing your own expectations is also critical. Hopefully, you've formed a sense of what you'd like to do next and have taken steps to pursue that path. Be sure not to expect too much too fast, and adjust your professional and financial expectations accordingly.

Finding a New Community

"When I was hired into my current job," explains William Lu (USN), "I was part of a cohort that included other veterans. We naturally gravitated to each other and formed a sort of clique in the company. Soon we found other veterans in the company and rebuilt a semblance of community that reminded us of what we'd left in the military." Lu found himself part of a diverse group with veterans from different branches of the military, of different ages and different jobs. What united them all was their military service.

A new community can provide you with much-needed support and encouragement in those first months and years on the job. Whether you all start your careers at the same time or have varying levels of experience, your community can help you navigate the complexities of onboarding and establishing your credibility with your team, supervisor, and colleagues.

You can also ask your community for help in navigating internal company systems and challenges. It may feel tempting to blurt out your objection to a project's budget forecast, but that could be seen as inappropriate coming from the "new gal" on the team. Your community can provide you with advice on what's appropriate and what's not appropriate in the job. Want approval to take a professional development course? Leverage your community's insight to understand the process to get what you want, from education, to promotions, to transfers within the company.

Asking for Help

Many of you will face a lot of decisions and choices. Perhaps you have several targeted employers you identify as "ideal," or maybe you receive several job offers and have to choose the one that's right for you. Or you get into every university you apply to and may not be sure which educational path to pursue. Asking for help, leveraging your connections, and tapping into formal and informal resources is invaluable as you start your post-military career. It may feel awkward to ask strangers to help you, but it's important to recognize that you cannot grow your career without the support, information, input, and resources others will provide you. As you were told in the military, "Embrace the suck." If the idea of asking for help is uncomfortable for you, I encourage you to embrace it regardless.

Lu describes this challenge this way: "When I left the military, I was not good at asking for help. I'd come from an environment where I was supposed to know everything, and if I didn't know it, I'd go look it up. Asking for help, showing my vulnerabilities, was a struggle as I made the transition. I learned, however, that when I could be genuine and ask others for guidance, resources, information, or help, they were more than willing to do so. This gave me a tremendous appreciation for mentoring as a way to get ahead in my career."

Creating Structure in Your Life and Each Day

Whether you're waiting until the school semester starts or you're building lists of potential investors to pitch on your business or you're in an active job search, you will stay productive and focused if you structure your day.

Create a daily routine that includes breaks and finishes at a reasonable hour each day to reinforce your skills of discipline, commitment, and focus. Wake up at a reasonable hour of the morning and follow a daily morning routine as if you were going to work or class. Instead of heading to an office or school, sit at the computer and review job openings, research potential employers, scour LinkedIn for new contacts for informational interviews, schedule time to speak with your mentor or advisor, follow up on resumes/interviews/meetings you've conducted, review/send resumes to new employers, and make lists of tasks you need to complete the following day. When you have a routine that keeps you focused, you are actively working on building your future and too busy to entertain doubts or anxieties.

In Closing

Starting your civilian career is not about accepting the first job you get and considering yourself set. When you evaluate opportunities, consider options, position yourself correctly, and accept chances to learn and grow, you can approach your career or academic or entrepreneurial pursuits with your eyes open.

Those first few years after the military will be filled with plot twists, surprises, and delights. Be careful about drawing premature conclusions about what they all mean—you may hit obstacles that are actually there to teach you something critical. You might be flooded with wonderful choices to hone your desires and goals. Learn to pause, reflect, consider, learn, and accept opportunities and challenges as gifts placed in your life to make you better.

Growing your career also means growing your community. Resist the temptation to isolate yourself. Instead ask for help, seek the companionship of others, and share your experiences. Community on campus, with other business owners, or in your first job is a critical factor to long-term success.

Growing Your Career in the First Three Years

11

Avoid hubris during your transition—life in the civilian sector won't be nirvana. Be careful when envisioning your new career.

—Doug Bartels

The first few years in your new career may feel like you're learning more in a short period of time than you did in your entire military career. At this point in your transition, you either have a job or are clear on what you're pursuing; you have the tools to either do your job or are learning how to acquire them; or you may be starting and maybe even completing school or starting a business.

Inventory What You've Learned So Far

Thinking back to the time you left your last duty station until now, inventory your findings to date. What important lessons have you gained? Are there aspects of the transition that caught you off guard? Are there relationships or opportunities that surprised you? How so?

Consider the skills, experiences, and training you've learned since leaving the military. Were these on-the-job lessons, online course work, or certifications you pursued and completed to help your career? What have you learned about yourself so far in the transition? Are you more resilient and self-disciplined than you believed? Are you more interested in global policy issues than you ever thought? Do you like to work in smaller groups? List what you've learned about yourself, getting as granular and personal as you possibly can.

You may realize that your work that doesn't align perfectly with your goals, personality, or values. A few years ago, I worked with Dana, a Marine who told me all she wanted was a management role in her government agency job. It's all she talked about and focused on. She truly believed that when she was a team manager, she'd have greater impact, influence, and job satisfaction. After three years in the job, Dana was finally promoted to manager. She was thrilled. Unfortunately, after only four months in management, Dana realized that what she'd wanted and strived for so hard for three years was not at all what she expected. As a manager, she spent most of her time focused on administrative responsibilities and navigating new relationships with colleagues. Her former colleagues who now reported to her viewed her differently. Overall, Dana was very unhappy at work. She learned the hard way that it's important to be clear about what you want and will strive to achieve.

Understanding Job Satisfaction, Purpose, and Meaning

"I didn't think it would be this hard." When Marc shared those sentiments with me, he sounded defeated and questioned his decision to leave the Army. "I was naive to think that my transition would be easier. I took my TAP classes online, exited the Army, and thought my ideal employer would be waiting for me in my hometown. The opposite has been true—I've had three jobs in two years, and none of them gave me the sense of fulfillment and purpose I had in the military."

Marc's sentiments are more typical than they are unique. Job satisfaction is not just about compensation and status. Duane France (USA, Ret.) today works as a mental health specialist, writing and speaking on the topic of post-military transition psychology. He notices that veterans often believe that, like work in the military, civilian work should provide both purpose and meaning. "Purpose," France explains, "is an external construct, a job to be done. In the military, your job may have been to pick up cigarette butts, and that was your purpose that day." He contrasts this notion with the understanding of meaning or finding meaningful work. "Meaning is an internal measure which gives us satisfaction and joy."

France notes that in the military, your work serves a distinct purpose but is meaningful to you and those you serve alongside. Your purpose serves the greater mission regardless of what the job is. After the military, it can be challenging to find both values in one job. Sometimes, he says, you have to find a job to pay the bills and a hobby that fulfills your need for meaningful impact or work.

As you evaluate job satisfaction in these first few critical years post-separation, consider whether your dissatisfaction is because you expect your day job to meet all your needs and goals. If your work is productive and purposeful and helps you to provide for yourself and your family but lacks meaning, consider outside involvement.

Check out nonprofit organizations like Team Rubicon, which utilizes the talents, skills, and experiences of military veterans to provide time-sensitive disaster relief globally. Or look into Team RWB, which connects veterans to their community through athletic and social activities. Both of these nonprofits (as well as many others) exist to help veterans find meaningful connection after the military.

Job Security Is a Myth

During a mentoring call with a transitioning soldier, he shared that he was thrilled that he'd landed his post-military job even before separating from the military. He told me he was set. He was going to be financially secure and was looking forward to spending the remainder of his working life as a management consultant with this large, global consulting firm.

I didn't want to burst his bubble, but the reality in today's workforce is that no job is completely safe and secure. Companies downsize and right size, contracts are lost, and clients fire companies, leading to reductions in workforce. Individuals who fall short of projected goals and expectations get fired. It's a mistake to assume you will have job security just because you get hired.

You may also decide to leave your job if you outgrow your current situation or if you want to pursue different work. Just as when you entered the military, you knew a day would come when you'd exit the military, the same holds for your first, second, and third jobs in the civilian sector.

Managing Your Career

Managing your post-military career will mean continuously building relationships and skills, taking advantage of opportunities that arise, averting or managing challenges that come up, and preparing for and driving opportunities that you've identified for your desired career path.

Assessing Your Progress on your Career Path: Adding Metrics

Take a moment and reflect on the past few months and years. Since you turned in your papers and began your transition, how do you feel the past few years has gone? Are you pleased with your progress to date? Are there things you wish you'd done differently?

It's healthy to assess your career satisfaction at various times over the next several years. This practice will help you figure out if you've progressed toward your goals. Create milestones that you can work toward. Where do you see yourself in three years? What skills would you like to add to your career portfolio? What promotions or advancements will you pursue? What kinds of responsibility will you want to have at work? Will you change jobs to increase your marketability or is staying with your current employer a smarter move for your career?

When you achieve these milestones, celebrate. Complete an after-action report at each milestone to assess what worked and didn't, where you learned and grew, and where you fell short. Continuing this practice will help you move forward and make progress over the entirety of your civilian career.

Evaluating Career Objectives and Nonnegotiables

You will also want to check in on the objectives and nonnegotiables you set earlier in your transition. If your goal was to be home for dinner with your family each night, how is that working? Are you seeing them three nights a week instead of seven? Is that acceptable? How about working on weekends? If you didn't set out to work a 70-hour week, are there aspects of the job that need to change, or do you need more training? This might be a good conversation with your boss.

If you strategically joined the company at a lower level or rank with the understanding that a step backward could move you forward faster, are you seeing signs of that forward momentum yet? Is there more you need to do to grow your role and contribution in the company? Again, having an honest and professional conversation with your boss can help make these goals more achievable.

Growing Your Career

While you may be new to the job, classroom, or entrepreneurial venture, it's important to continually grow your career by adding experiences, knowledge, and hard and soft skills. One client I worked with was happy in his job in a boutique investment firm but realized much of the professional terminology that he heard in casual conversations, investor pitches, and even meetings with his boss was still foreign to him. He enrolled in a community college and took business courses, found additional classes online, and watched YouTube tutorials about the investment community. Seek outside training or education to ensure your skills and knowledge are on par with your peers.

Keep Asking for Help

You've heard it before, but in these first few years after exiting the military, asking for help is very important. If you don't understand something at work, ask your peers, boss, mentor, anyone for guidance and assistance. Remember, asking for help is a sign of strength, not weakness.

Your mentor should be an active part of your life and career in these years. Whether you meet with them regularly or check in periodically, you should rely on your mentor to help you navigate questions at work, challenges in your career plan, or obstacles in your personal life. Your mentor wants you to succeed.

If you feel overwhelmed and are struggling, don't be afraid to seek professional help. Duane France, mentioned earlier, notes, "If you go through five deployments, you'll likely have some dents in your fender." Whether you served in combat or not, whether you served a year or 30, this transition requires you to navigate unknown territory. When in doubt, seek help. If you feel overwhelmed, frustrated, anxious, depressed, or angry, look for assistance. Don't try to solve the problems yourself when there are professionals waiting to help.

Keep Up Your Networking

By now your network likely includes new groups of people including individuals you know at work, in the industry, clients and prospects, and other veteran community members. Make sure these relationships are valuable to you and to your network. Maybe you don't need help finding a job, but you'd like insight into a new client opportunity. Your network can help you here. Perhaps you're graduating school soon and seek connections for your first full-time, post-military job or internship. Maybe now your business plan is fleshed out and you're ready to look outside of friends and family for investment funding—again, your network can provide guidance and connections.

You may also find that now you've become a more valuable asset to your network. With a few years of work experience, a well-developed and growing personal brand, and new connections, you could be in a more influential position to help and assist your network. This can change the complexion of your relationships for the better.

Some ways you'll stay connected with your network include:

- **Conscious networking.** As you grow your civilian career, your network will grow as well. You'll certainly build your network faster if you are less discerning about who gets included, but you could risk losing the integrity of your relationships or degrading the quality of your connections. If you follow a more conscious practice of networking, you'll thoughtfully add connections as they make sense for you and the contact. At each opportunity, ask yourself: How can this person help me? How can I help them? Are there risks to the relationship? What are the benefits? Add connections online and in person that grow your career well into the future.

Networking requires long-term investment and nurturing to remain valuable. Long after you land the job, start and finish school, or build and sell your company, you should engage with your network. Nurturing the relationship might mean face-to-face meetings periodically or quick phone calls to update each other a few times a year. Other connections may be content to see your updates on LinkedIn to feel informed about your career and goals. You'll have to judge which approach makes the most sense, based on the expectations of the relationship, their value to you in your career, and your willingness to nurture the connection.

- **Accountability partner.** It is helpful to have someone to hold you accountable to the decisions you make and the vision you pursue. An accountability partner can be your mentor, friend, coach, peer, or manager. Their role is to understand your goals and check in with you to evaluate your progress. My accountability partners check in with me to ask how I'm progressing toward my goals and offer ideas or suggestions when I need it. Consider being mutually accountable with a peer or friend, where you can support each other as you grow your careers.

- **Volunteering.** We know that your desire to serve does not end when you leave the military. For many of you, your work will fulfill your sense of duty and provide meaningful ways of serving communities you're passionate about. For others of you, volunteering outside of work will meet these needs. Consider nonprofit organizations that not only interest you and support your passions, but where your skills and talents will be valued and utilized. If your skills are in marketing or recruiting, consider joining the fundraising team on a local nonprofit. Handy with a hammer and nail gun? Why not build homes for an organization focused on ending homelessness? Talented with understanding policy and laws? Many organizations could benefit from your expertise as they seek to impact legislation for the constituents they serve.

- **Mentoring.** When you want to give back, consider mentoring another veteran at work or through a mentoring platform or a civilian who could benefit from your experience, lessons learned, and connections. David Resilien, a former Marine Corps Gunnery Sergeant, found mentoring to be a way to stay connected to his military life. "I was able to share my experiences with service members who would go through what I'd been through," says Resilien. "I'd missed interacting with my fellow service members, and mentoring kept me connected to my military life." Today Resilien mentors veterans on aspects of the transition he experienced firsthand, including planning career moves, setting goals, and life adjustments.

Pursuing Side Jobs for Extra Income

If an assessment of your current job situation reveals that you're below the income threshold you anticipated, consider side work. The gig economy, as it's called, is growing as individuals find themselves drawn to nontraditional jobs to either supplement their income or take them out of traditional jobs entirely.

Gig jobs are part-time, flexible positions, such as driving for an on-demand car service, babysitting, pet walking, or freelance and contract work. The income is less predictable and steady, but you can work gig jobs to pay off bills, supplant your income, or save for vacation. Before embarking on side jobs, make sure your employer knows and does not see any conflict of interest with your primary job.

Advancing Your Career: Seeking a Promotion

Imagine you learned of a job opening in your team that offered more responsibility, visibility, and pay. This type of advancement, or promotion, typically requires you apply for the position, interview, and, if selected, possibly train your replacement as you learn your new role.

To pursue a promotion in your own (or another) department in your company, you'll have to research the opportunity. In the same way you researched the company before being hired, you'll now want to investigate the new opportunity for its benefits and risks. Learn all you can about the new team, their goals and programs, and how your skills and experiences meet those goals.

There are pros and cons to alerting your boss of your intentions, so decide whether to have a conversation with your boss in advance of your application if the position is outside your current department or team. On the negative side, your boss could question your loyalty to the team or project, sabotage your chances by sharing bad information, or begin distancing from you in anticipation of your leaving. On the positive side, your boss could be a tremendous advocate for you, providing you with insight and information about the new team and project, supporting and coaching you through the interview, and singing your praises to the decision makers in hiring.

Interviewing for the Promotion

In preparing for an internal job interview—a promotion or transfer within your current employer—begin by inventorying your skills, qualifications, and advantages to pursue the promotion. Just because you currently work for the company does not mean you're automatically their first choice. In many cases, companies like to bring in outside people for their fresh ideas and perspectives or their competitive intelligence.

Take stock of your knowledge of the company mission, vision, and growth. Inventory the relationships you have with key influencers who can vouch for your accomplishments and impact at the company during your tenure. Solicit feedback on how you're perceived so you have the insight to promote yourself favorably to the decision makers for the open position.

Treat the interview for an internal job the same as you would an external interview. Align your experience to job responsibilities and demonstrate your understanding of the business and vision for the new position.

How to Respond If You Get Promoted

Congratulations, you got the promotion. Before you gloat, remember that your coworkers may have mixed feelings about your success. Perhaps one of them also applied for the new job. Maybe they're sad to see you move out of the team and are concerned about the gap your absence will create.

Discuss how you will handle the transition with your boss. Are there ways to ensure a smooth transition? Will you be training your replacement? How can you create an optimal outcome from this move for the team you're leaving and the one you're moving to, if you're changing departments?

Handling Rejection (If You Didn't Get the Promotion)

Although you might believe the entire team knew you were interviewing, in fact, they may not. In that case, you can decide whether to tell them you were striving for a new opportunity or remain quiet. What's most important is that you return to your current role with the same commitment and enthusiasm as you had when first hired. Your boss will be watching for signs of frustration or sour grapes and will want to fend off any toxicity you might bring back to the team.

Use the opportunity to solicit feedback, if possible. Ask why you didn't get the promotion, what you did well, and what you could have done better. This will help you position yourself better the next time an opportunity arises.

Handling Career Setbacks and Challenges

You will undoubtedly experience career setbacks along the way. Whether you chose the wrong job because it paid really well, or you didn't ask enough questions before leading a key project, setbacks happen. What matters most is how you handle it. "I wish I'd asked better questions," remarked a Marine I mentored. "I took what my boss said at face value and never thought I could probe deeper or offer an alternative direction for my career path."

Remember that you are in charge of your career and your professional growth now. When things go awry, connect with your mentors, coaches, and advisors. They've been through what you're experiencing and often can help you navigate the turbulent waters. Trust their judgment but filter their advice through your own decision-making tools. Ask yourself:

- Am I responding out of fear or discomfort?
- Am I growing and learning (and that feels odd)?
- Could I have prevented this situation? If so, how?
- What, in my current situation, is outside of my control?
- What am I learning through this process?

The point is not to avoid all stress and challenge but to create and use the tools that will help you successfully navigate tough times.

Receiving on-the-Job Feedback

Performance reviews and appraisals are commonplace in most businesses and organizations. These assessments offer the employer an opportunity to evaluate your work and progress, identify areas for improvement or growth, and correct any problems or challenges before they become worse. A manager will also work with employees to set new or revised goals during a performance review. In some cases, managers will create a performance plan where the employee must improve in specific areas or be terminated.

Mike found his first corporate job performance review disheartening. He started working for a large, international technology company eight months after leaving the Army. He thought he was doing well. His boss never corrected him, he learned many new systems and applications on the job, attended an off-site training program offered to him, and even had a few friends at work. However, during the formal review, his boss shared some disturbing comments from Mike's peers, coworkers in other departments, and even a few clients. Mike scored a "below expectations" on his overall job skills evaluation, and the comments painted him as someone who was bossy, stubborn, noncollaborative, and lacked commitment to the project's overall mission. It turns out Mike was not well liked within the company.

As a result of this feedback, Mike was demoted. His first reaction was to quit or at least threaten to leave. He'd done everything he was told to do, and he did it efficiently. What Mike missed, however, was the relational aspects of the job. Although he did his tasks at a satisfactory level, the way he did them bothered other people and made Mike unpleasant to be around.

Instead of quitting in a huff, Mike took a step back to reassess. He really liked the company and the industry and valued his colleagues and the mission they all worked toward. A conversation with his mentor helped Mike see that he needed to reframe some of his narrative from the military work style, understand the civilian culture and the unwritten norms and goals, and find a way to rebuild trust.

Performance reviews also provide employees with an opportunity to share concerns, ask for guidance, and offer feedback to their managers. Just as managers will structure their comments with thought and care, so should employees. A performance review is not the opportunity to unleash pent-up complaints but rather to showcase how things could be better.

Whenever you're offered feedback, guidance, or insight, view it as helpful information. Feedback can tell you if you're on the right track and valued by the company and your peers. It can also provide guidance so you can improve and retain your job. Does the feedback you're hearing confirm that you are moving closer to your desired reputation? Are the words used to describe you the ones you want to be known by? Or, if the feedback is highlighting a gap between how you want to be known and how you're perceived, are you motivated to make changes to correct the situation?

Just because you're offered feedback doesn't mean you have to act on it or modify your behavior. The person offering the feedback may have skewed or faulty information. You might receive feedback that feels overly personal or cruel. In some cases, the feedback points to overwhelming challenges that are better solved by changing where you work. For now, remember that where the feedback offers you an opportunity to better yourself and the career you seek, it's valuable. When it's not helpful or takes you off course, it might be wise to ignore.

Building and Managing Relationships at Work

Since job advancement is not predictable, relationships with your boss, peers, coworkers, clients, vendors, and others matter. Your boss may help you navigate your career at the company, your peers can offer insight about your performance, and others can help provide opportunities that help you advance outside of work.

Communicating with Your Boss: Having Honest Conversations

There may be times when you need to share bad news with your boss. Doing this can be tricky. When handled correctly, an honest conversation with your boss can produce great results and build your credibility.

Consider how you would relate bad news to your boss. If you can't meet a deadline, is it because of factors outside of your control? Or did you mismanage your time? As clearly as you can, strip out the emotion or judgment of the situation to see the facts. Then imagine your boss's position and perspective. Is this project critical to your boss's career at the company? What's at stake for the boss if you miss the deadline? Then research options to solve the issue or resolve the situation before you approach your boss. Is there a way to fix things? If so, have a list of suggestions ready to discuss in person with your boss or to share in writing if you can't meet in person.

When asking for a conversation with your boss, try to meet in person. If you work remotely or travel a lot, try for a video call or phone call. This ensures that body language and tonality of voice will help deliver the message.

After you've presented the situation, empathize with how this information impacts your boss and offer viable options and solutions. Be sure to ask your boss about next steps, but respect that your boss might need time to consider the situation. Your boss may not be able to give you an answer or definitive response on the spot.

Getting Along with Your Coworkers

What makes some people popular at work? Does their likability and favorable reputation give them a career advantage? Jennifer, a Coast Guard veteran, described a situation she couldn't reconcile. She'd been on the team at her new company for about 18 months when Adam was transferred into her department to help with a big contract the team had won. Jennifer had been key to winning the work and wanted the team to understand all the risks involved in moving forward on the project. But Adam was jovial, affable, and social and often made people laugh. Soon he was given the lead on the project, even though his experience and skills were not up to par. Adam often asked for deadline extensions, was late to meetings, and occasionally made comments Jennifer found off-putting. Yet he continued to get more responsibility as the project grew. Jennifer could not comprehend how someone with suboptimal skills was so well regarded by the team and by their manager. "Was his cheerful personality the key to his career success?" she asked.

The civilian sector is relational, and companies hire and promote for culture, fit, and contribution. It's not a linear process where you check all the boxes and a promotion is forthcoming. How you are perceived by your coworkers and supervisors matters.

In Adam's case, he'd built such favorable relationships with his peers that they overlooked his shortcomings and even covered for him when he missed a deadline. His manager looked past his tardiness because he added joy and levity to meetings. Yes, his manager pulled Adam aside a few times and counseled him on the appropriateness of some of his jokes, but overall his behavior was tolerated.

Jennifer, in contrast, repeatedly played devil's advocate, pointing out risks and possible exposure for the team. Although her messages were appropriate and valuable, her delivery lacked finesse and warmth. The company valued itself as a happy workplace where leaders were selected for their ability to contribute but also to add to the cultural goals.

I've often said, "Your attitude is your altitude." This means that your ability to soar high into the ranks of management sometimes is determined by how you see the world and how you communicate that view is. When you are viewed as a leader and team player and someone others want to work with, opportunities open up. Right or wrong, people like to do business with people they like.

Managing Up and Across the Company: Understanding Chain of Command

Management in a civilian company or organization will feel very different from leadership in the military. Companies strive to build leaders who will inspire, collaborate with, and cultivate a thriving, happy workforce, but they still require managers to handle administrative, budgetary, and supervisory duties.

In your role, you'll seek to influence others across the company. Communicating your vision or concerns with someone outside your rank may have been frowned on in the military, working cross-functionally within a civilian company is normal. It is not unusual to approach managers in other departments to gain buy-in or assistance.

Growing your value within the company means reaching for and using all available levers to promote your vision, support your team, and advance the company's mission. Once you have a firm understanding of the company culture, written and unwritten norms, and personalities, you should seek relationships that extend beyond the obvious chain of command. Your direct manager is not the only decision-making power.

Consider this scenario: You are project lead on an assignment that requires input from other teams in the company. You have a manager who ensures you meet deadlines and deliverables in the project plan. But you also have an internal customer who owns the project and another department lead who oversees all similar initiatives. In this case, your manager approves your paycheck, your internal client approves your work, and the other department lead approves the company taking on the project with you as lead. Each of these bosses has an impact on your career success. You may believe you are accountable only to your direct boss, but these other clients and leads will need to see and appreciate your value just as much.

Adding Extra Value Throughout Your Career: Lagniappe

There's a term a client shared with me when describing his desire to always give more than he gets: lagniappe (pronounced lan-yap). The term's origin may have been Louisiana-French or Mark Twain, scholars aren't sure. But it describes the little something extra one gives to another. For example, the baker's dozen is actually 13 donuts, not 12 as the word "dozen" implies. The extra one is lagniappe. When someone goes above and beyond in an unexpected way, it's called lagniappe.

Throughout your career, look for ways to add lagniappe to your work. Go the extra mile, find the extra value, add the extra donut. Giving more than what's expected will never feel like waste. The benefits might not be immediate or obvious, but the impact of your contribution and generosity will be felt by the population or person who needs it.

In Closing

Growing your post-military career is not just about a new employer and paycheck. It's about finding a new culture, set of values, and system to work within to find meaning and impact. Whether you're going from the front line or the office, from combat to executive leadership, your transition will be a very personal process. Be careful comparing yourself to those around you because you'll never know the variables and circumstances that lead others to make the choices they are making. Focus on yourself and what is in alignment with your values and goals for your career and life.

The first few years after separation or retirement can feel like a blur. Nothing may seem predictable or routine, and you may experience more change in three years than you did with all of your military assignments combined. You'll be navigating unfamiliar situations and may feel unprepared for the challenges you face. Realize that these years are formational. They help set the foundation for the rest of your civilian career.

In the same way that runners don't look down but ahead during a marathon, keep your focus on the tasks and goals in front of you. Stay true to the goals you set initially, and remind yourself of the impact you seek to make to keep yourself motivated through this next stage of your career.

Growing Your Career and Knowing When to Move On

12

You will face a lot of changes over the course of your post-military career. You will face job changes, company changes, team changes, and more. Whether and how you learn to navigate these changes will determine whether you succumb or thrive.

Once you accept that change is inevitable, you can focus your energy on developing the skills to adapt to, overcome, and thrive in new circumstances. Making a commitment to continual growth and self-improvement will help you manage the evolution of your work and career.

Along with a positive mindset and attitude, it's important to maintain the work you've done so far in developing your professional skills. Take advantage of the numerous books, seminars, online courses, trainings, coaches, and other professional development tools to grow your civilian career over the long term.

Part of growing professionally is learning when it's time for you to move on. This can be one of the hardest decisions to make, particularly in the early years. Let's examine the options and factors to consider.

When the Job Isn't Working Out

There are many reasons jobs don't work out. Poor timing, poor job choice, and poor culture fit can all lead to job dissatisfaction and unhappiness. When you've considered all options and remedies and decided a change is warranted, there's a right (and a wrong) way to quit your job. Before making the change, you need to learn how to make the decision to quit, how to navigate the timing of your announcement, and how to handle the communications around your decision.

It's important to note that mental health issues often present as job challenges. If you feel you are wrestling with challenges in your emotional outlook or mental health, seek the advice and care of a trained professional. Fortunately, discussing issues surrounding the topic of mental health is more acceptable today than it was in the past, and there is no stigma attached to seeking treatment or counseling. Remember, asking for help is a sign of strength.

Recognize When You Need to Change Jobs

Let's consider how the following individuals thought through the decision to stay or leave:

"I'm paid well for the work I do," Mark told me. "I feel like I can't leave this job, even though I hate going to work every day. I'm just not inspired anymore."

"I convinced them to hire me," said Sarah, "I made the choice to accept the job, knowing what I was getting into. It wouldn't be fair to leave this job after just a year. I need to stick with my commitment and honor my word."

"Everything about my job changed over the past year," notes Anthony. "I've had three bosses in the past 12 months, the project I was hired to lead got put on hold, and they've cut all expense reimbursements, meaning I have to pay for my own materials out of my own paycheck. But if I quit, I'd look like I'm deserting my team. I can't do that to them."

These are all real scenarios. Even after you leave the military, you may still carry the sense of fairness, loyalty, service, and commitment that drew you to military service in the first place. You may find that the hardest career challenge is putting yourself first over the needs of the company or team.

Although your situation and circumstances may look very different than those outlined, there are factors to be considered other than your feelings of disenchantment with your employer. Mark, Sarah, and Anthony all wanted to leave their roles, but leaving wasn't their only option. Let's consider their situations in a little more depth.

In Mark's case, he was well compensated for the work he did. He was hired into a position where his skills and talents would be fully utilized, and things went well for a while. Then he lost interest. He lost his momentum, enthusiasm, and inspiration for the job, his co-workers, and the company mission.

Mark had some other opportunities to explore. Because he liked the company and its culture, he could meet with his boss and explore additional ways to grow his role and influence in the company. He could look at other opportunities within the company that might offer him greater growth potential. He could also seek more "inspiring" volunteer work outside of his job. Before quitting, Mark would be advised to investigate and consider the options.

In Sarah's case, she felt a combination of loyalty and guilt because she believed she'd somehow tricked her employer into hiring her. Sarah's loyalty was not misplaced. Her boss was happy with her progress and the value she brought to the company and her team. The company was willing to invest more to train Sarah in new technologies and skills to enhance her contribution. It also wanted to expose her to increasingly complex client projects and offer her an opportunity to lead a women veterans' group within the company. Instead of quitting, Sarah could discuss her dissatisfaction with her boss and explore options within the company. If she still felt she needed to make a change, she could do so in a way that maintains her integrity and credibility with her employer.

In Anthony's situation, there were red flags all around. He thought the company was stable, even on a growth trajectory. Once onboard, he learned that it was floundering. The company had attempted a few strategic mergers, completed a wholesale change in executive leadership, and struggled to realign the company culture with their business vision. Anthony was in a firestorm.

Anthony's frustration with constantly changing bosses and irritation with financial restrictions that impeded his ability to do his job, and his overall lack of enthusiasm for the company's future led him to the decision to work elsewhere. Because of the unstable nature of Anthony's employer, he would be advised to make a discreet job search to avoid a sudden reactive firing from his employer.

Why You Might Want to Leave Your Current Employer

There are a few common reasons why people decide to leave their jobs, including bad leadership, wrong job, lack of training, bad fit with company or culture or work, and a lack of advancement potential.

- **Bad leadership.** Numerous studies of workplace satisfaction find that employees mostly leave companies because of poor leadership and management rather than because of compensation or work. Employees may feel they aren't given clear and practical guidance, or they don't feel supported and encouraged at work.

- **Wrong job.** Were you hired into a position that truly was below your capabilities, skills, and talent? Is there no road to upward mobility in the company? Are you woefully underpaid for your contribution? Workers often accept jobs that don't fully utilize their skills and then find themselves frustrated and unsatisfied in their work.

- **Lack of training.** Did you choose a job in which you needed to develop new skills in an attempt to launch a career in a new field? Are you lacking the skills and training to do the work? It's important to feel empowered and qualified to do the work you're hired to do. Otherwise, each day on the job can feel like another step backward, not forward, in your career.

- **Bad fit with company or culture or work.** This happens. Jobs or companies that might appear attractive may fail to meet your expectations after you start working. Sometimes it's how we get along, sometimes it's the fact that most people don't like working there, and sometimes we just don't fit in.

- **Lack of advancement potential.** Some companies artificially create ceilings past which you can't ascend. If you have repeatedly applied for internal promotions, volunteered for additional work, or even pursued additional training to grow your skills and been rejected, it might be time for you to move on. Sometimes moving on is the only way to advance your career.

Fear Versus Discomfort

Before making the decision to leave, ask yourself if you are motivated to leave out of discomfort or out of fear. If you decide to leave because you're afraid or feel unsafe, you need to pay attention. Fear is a real emotion that comes when we perceive danger, inappropriateness, or threat.

Discomfort can create feelings similar to fear, but the cause of discomfort is not life-threatening. Discomfort in a role may cause you to feel anxious or worried—as fear does—but the anxiety or unsettled feeling could be a signal that you're growing, learning, and stretching. In that case, discomfort can be a great thing. For example, you might have felt uncomfortable when we discussed personal branding. You were being asked questions that moved you out of your comfort zone, causing you to reflect on issues, values, and behaviors that may not have been positive and stretched your thinking about how you need to behave and communicate going forward. But you went through the uncomfortable experience because you knew you were still safe. You were learning and growing.

When you begin a new exercise routine, you are using new muscles, and those new muscles respond by becoming sore, tight, and resistant. But over time, those muscles become stronger, and exercising becomes easier and less painful. Consider that what you're feeling may be the sensation of working a new set of muscles, not something to fear.

Before you quit your current job, consider the cause of your discomfort. Are you working on projects that are unfamiliar? Are you using skills you haven't fully developed? Are you being asked to collaborate with peers who are very different from you? Is this discomfort caused by something unhealthy, inappropriate, or threatening, or are you developing new skills and experiences that ultimately will make you stronger and healthier?

Optics Matter in a Job Change

When the job you applied for, interviewed for, negotiated, accepted, and poured your heart into isn't what you wanted, it can feel devastating. You might feel like you failed by choosing the wrong job or mismanaged your priorities.

In any job change, you should pay attention to how your move appears to others. Whether you are changing career situations as an employee, entrepreneur, or student, how you are seen behaving, handling relationships, and managing communications matters. Those around you will form perceptions and opinions about your thought process as you chose to make a change and decide whether they would do the same if in your situation. If you leave your job in a furry of expletives, slamming doors behind you, consider what message that sends to your former colleagues. If you put school/college on hold and disappear from social media, leaving your peers to worry about you, what does that say about your thought processes? It's not a good look.

Too many job changes can also be warning signs for potential employers who review your resume. If your resume reflects a history of many short-term jobs without an acceptable narrative to explain all the changes, potential employers could perceive you as a high risk. Entrepreneurs who start multiple businesses can be seen as innovative and risk taking, they also can be perceived as impetuous and unfocused. And a student who frequently changes majors or drops out of school without explanation may be perceived as undisciplined and lacking in direction.

Although you shouldn't live your life concerned wholly with how others view you, your reputation is based on other people's perception of you. And when you are trying to grow your career, reputation matters.

Going from Entrepreneur to Employee

Let's say you left the military with a business plan and an initial investment in hand and charged forward into the world of business ownership. You persevered through the hardships of the startup stage, such as getting the business license, loans or other funding, marketing, product prototyping, and securing those first few clients. But now you realize you want to do something else, perhaps because you lost interest in the business or faced unplanned personal hardships, or because the competition grew too fierce.

Many entrepreneurs find themselves closing the business and pivoting to new careers. If you've come to the decision to leave business ownership and join a company as an employee, you'll need to manage the narrative and explanation of that move carefully.

To create the basis of your narrative, think about what you experienced during your time in the military and as an entrepreneur. For each stage in your career, list the skills, experiences, and lessons that you will use to help you in your new career. Consider the following questions.

- Why did you join the military? What was your motivation?
- Why did you leave the military? What was your motivation?
- What appealed to you about starting a business?
- What did you do well as a business owner?
- What led you to close the business?

The point of this exercise is to identify your motivations and look for behavior patterns that can be used to figure out what to do next. This exercise can also help you craft your narrative so you can explain to an employer why you're making a change from business owner to employee.

Let's say that you joined the military because you felt a sense of duty to serve after the events of September 11, 2001. Joining the military helped you respond to the feelings of helplessness most Americans felt when we were attacked at home. Maybe you left the military so you could have freedom over your income and lifestyle and discovered that you were really good at flipping houses. You started your own business and could work anywhere in the country. After a while perhaps you learned that, although you love to work on houses and you loved the money you'd made on your first few flips, it was exhausting work. Having to raise capital while you waited for each property to sell, combined with a turbulent housing market and the challenge of finding a reliable construction crew grew too burdensome.

What patterns emerge from this example? For one, this individual cares about freedom—freedom from financial burdens, independent working (outside and on houses), and traveling across the country. Because this person served in the military and then led a construction crew, it also appears that this person also likes to manage and lead others. In moving to a next job, this veteran would be advised to highlight the skills and experiences that have helped in their careers so far. The veteran might highlight a passion for growth, hard work, entrepreneurship, and resilience. This person might also consider a position that involves travel. A job in sales could be a great fit for this veteran-entrepreneur-employee as he or she continues to pursue financial independence and career growth.

Whatever patterns emerge, what matters most is that you control the narrative. You need to help an employer understand why your background and experience qualify you for the opportunity that is on offer. You can't afford to assume than an employer would find your experiences valuable.

When School Doesn't Work Out

With the costs of higher education skyrocketing, many traditional students are evaluating the decision to go to college or graduate school rather than join the ranks of the employed. As a veteran, you likely have leveraged your post-9/11 GI Bill benefits to offset school and housing costs as you pursue a degree.

If you are thinking about leaving school because the academic path is no longer providing what it offered initially or is no longer viable, you will want to control the narrative. You will need to explain to potential employers why you left school and how you will use what you learned there to increase your value as an employee. As you create a narrative, consider these questions.

- What led you to the military?
- What did you do in the military?
- Why did you leave the military?

- What attracted you to college and the program you chose?
- What did you learn/do well while in school?
- Why are you leaving school before completing your degree?

Let's say you joined the military because you saw a path to getting an education and serving your country. Upon entering the military, you realized you liked working with your hands. You became a mechanic and then began teaching soldiers the fundamentals of mechanics. After six years, you realized you wanted to go to college full-time outside of the military so you could work in a trade. You majored in business so you could open an automobile repair shop one day. However, you grew tired of classes and homework and learned that you really enjoyed being a mechanic and weren't as interested in running a business.

From this example, you can see a few patterns. This individual likes to learn, work with their hands, teach others, and see things fixed or built. The person is less interested in theory and more in the mechanical applications of work. If this person pursued a career in the auto repair trade, he or she could eventually seek a teaching role in a trade school or manage a repair shop. Again, whatever the particulars of the story might be, the patterns are what helps you craft you narrative that you can share with prospective employers.

Making Your Career Change

After evaluating your reasons for making a change but before you publicly announce it, discuss the move with your support system and consider what you want to do next. Hopefully the process of making this decision has helped you figure out what made you unhappy, and you can now move ahead with a better idea of what will bring meaningful employment.

If the reasons you weren't advancing in your job or being recommended for key projects is due to your lack of education or training, perhaps the time is right to get that done. Maybe you weren't happy because you truly want to run your own business. Is the time right for self-employment or entrepreneurship?

Remove any false pretenses ("I'm just too valuable not to be promoted" or "They're idiots for not seeing how important I am"), and think clearly and realistically as you set the strategy for making your next career move. You will think about this move differently from your first post-military choice. You now have a job on your resume, and what comes next continues the story you started. Too many random, disconnected, or seemingly incongruous jobs after the military can paint the picture of someone unfocused or unstable. You'll need to choose your next move strategically.

Before You Quit: Talk to Your Boss

Regardless of why you want to leave, it's important to explore all options first even if it's simply because you want it to look like you tried before quitting. Consider having an honest conversation with your boss before turning in your resignation or making an announcement. Doing this will help you to determine if there's a possibility of improving your current situation. If there is not, this method allows you to show professional good face by going to your boss first before quitting.

Be sure you do your homework. If you're leaving because you are unhappy with the compensation and pay, look at salaries at other companies in your area for the same work. If you're leaving because you feel you aren't moving quickly enough in your career at the company, list out all the ways in which you've added exceptional value and that would warrant advancement. Be clear and specific in your explanation of your decision.

If you're leaving because you simply don't like the job or the company, be clear about this too. You want to communicate why the job or company wasn't a good match for you without being destructive and offensive. You may have had different expectations, or your needs and goals might have changed. Be respectful and professional. You may encounter this company and individual again in your professional life so you don't want to burn bridges. If you're open to other opportunities in the company, let your boss know. This could start the process of internal interviewing for another job in the same company.

Work with your boss on a transition plan. Let the person know you're willing to help move any programs and projects of yours to your colleagues, and you'll exit gracefully. Understand that your boss may want you to leave the company that day. This is not an unusual request; some employers fear you'll taint the team or project if you stay. Be prepared to have your employment end the very day you talk to your boss.

Before You Quit: Talk to Your Support System

Discuss your frustrations or disappointments with your family, and let them know that you are considering a change. You will want them to support you through the process. Evaluate your financial situation and goals, and plan your move so you can continue to meet your family's needs and obligations. You don't want to pick a bad time to quit. Review your thinking and decision with your mentors too. Let them run what-if scenarios by you to ensure you've considered all possibilities before quitting your job. Listen as they offer insight and ideas. Remember, they're your mentors because of their wisdom and insight. Use it.

Before You Quit: Explore Options at the Company First

If the reason you're looking to leave the company is because you're not happy at work, consider what it is about the job you dislike and why. For instance, if you exited the military at a senior officer rank and suddenly find yourself in a company where you need to complete your own expense reports, arrange your own travel, and set your own meetings, this can feel wildly unfamiliar. Consider the options that exist in your current situation before just pulling the plug. Is preparing your own expense reports really that cumbersome (or is it the idea of the task that bothers you)? Can you get administrative support? See what options exist in your current role to improve your situation before you assume there are none.

In addition to finding ways to improve your current situation, explore opportunities in other departments in the company. If you were hired into a project management role but find your interests more closely align with the marketing team, inquire about opportunities to transfer to that team and grow from there.

It is costly and time consuming to hire employees. If you are a valuable contributor to your company, it may be motivated to work with you to improve your current situation or move you to another team in order to retain your talent, experience, and knowledge.

What If You Don't Know What You Want Next?

If you aren't sure of what you want next but you know you don't want this, then your transition may be trickier. You may still have the conversation with your boss, and the outcome may be to take on more or less responsibility or to get more training or even transfer to another department in the company. All of this may solve your job dissatisfaction, or it can help buy you time.

Restart Your Informational Interviews

Informational interviews are helpful at this stage. If you're not sure what to do next or if you have an idea but need help figuring out the path, set up time to meet with people in your network whose work, company, or life experience is interesting to you. Create a set of questions to ask them to help discern what, if anything, they all have in common, and use that information to create your action plan for a new job.

Your network will be invaluable to you as you figure out what to do next. Hopefully you've stayed in touch with the people you did informational interviews with to secure your first post-military job. Now's a good time to connect with them and, if their insights are valuable to you where you are, revisit an informational interview with them. If not, find people in your network who have insights, information, and guidance to help you move forward in your civilian career.

Your informational interview will be different this time around. You'll have had the benefit of spending some time in the civilian sector working alongside different types of people and in different environments and cultures. You'll have a clearer sense of what you want and don't want, what you like and dislike, and how you want to add value to an organization. Keep this in mind as you seek their input and insight into options, risks, rewards, and considerations as you exit your current employment. Your credibility with these contacts can help you seek introductions and connections as they support your vision for your next career.

How to Quit Your Job Gracefully

To exit your current situation and enter a new path with professionalism and credibility, I suggest the following.

1 **Recognize how you got here.** Did you oversell your skills and experience when interviewing for this job? Were you seduced by a good sales pitch on the company's future and your potential and ended up in a disappointing arrangement? Recognizing the problem will help ensure you don't repeat the same behavior going forward.

2 **Review the terms of your employment agreement before talking to a competitor or client.** It might feel easiest to speak to your company's main competitor or largest client about a new job, but you may have signed a noncompete or nondisclosure agreement, which would make this a bad move. Review all the paperwork you signed and received during your hiring and onboarding before pursuing opportunities.

3 **Consider the timing.** Although companies understand that employees leave jobs for different reasons, they are not fond of employees abandoning projects at critical junctures. Consider whether you'd earn more credibility with your supervisors and team if you see the project through. Evaluate market timing (is the economy headed for a recession?) and whether your dream employer may be headed into a hiring freeze. In some cases, it's advised to stay put until conditions improve.

4 Job search on your time. Update your resume, contact your online networks, and conduct your informational interviews when you're not on your employer's clock. Conduct these activities on your lunch break or after work.

5 Be careful when posting on social media. Unless you've given notice at work and your job search is public, be careful posting and applying to jobs on public sites. Similarly, if your job search is not public, be careful applying to jobs where the employer's name is hidden. This could be your current employer, and now you've revealed your intention to leave. This can hasten your departure if employers suspect you aren't loyal to the company or job any longer.

6 Understand your compensation benefits. Have you accrued paid time off, sick pay, or floating holidays? When you leave, some of this may be paid to you and some may revert back to the employer. Consider how you might use these benefits to conduct your job search (interviewing, meetings, etc.) and what you'll lose if you leave prematurely. For instance, if you received a hiring bonus or moving expenses as part of your hire, and the agreement states you'll have to repay those expenses if you quit within a certain time frame, you might consider sticking with the job a few more months.

7 Give appropriate advance notice. Employers don't like sudden exits from key employees. Such departures can leave teams, projects, and other departments shorthanded. Plan to offer at least two weeks' notice to help transition your work or train your replacement.

Remember that your employer may ask you to leave the day you give notice of your intent to leave. Employers may believe that your work quality will suffer if you stay or that you may take company information with you. Be prepared in advance for this to happen so you aren't caught off guard if you're escorted out after quitting.

8 Line up another job first. Whenever possible, have your next job lined up before you quit. Employment gaps can be a red flag for potential employers, and some employers find it more attractive to recruit someone currently in a job rather than someone who's unemployed.

Finding the Next Job

You already know that social networking, resumes and cover letters, and networking connections are crucial ingredients to a meaningful career. Now, as you search for another job, you'll deploy them again to target your next employer and opportunity.

While you are still employed, update your resume and social networking platforms (i.e., LinkedIn) with all the results, impacts, accomplishments, and successes of your current job. If you are changing industries or areas of focus within the industry (e.g., business development to sales or supply chain management to operations), then update the keywords in your job description and profile as well. Employers will search for you while you're still employed, so updating the description of what you're currently doing to attract them is a good strategy.

Focus on your networking efforts now too. Increase your face time with your contacts by meeting for lunch or coffee to reconnect and update them on your goals. Attend more social and business gatherings, reminding the people you connect with how they can help you. If you're changing industries or jobs, consider attending relevant events. If you attended construction events because you worked in construction management but now will pursue a residential real estate career, attend meetings, events, and seminars where real estate agents and buyers network. This helps entrench you in your new community.

Be sure to let your online network know that you'll be making a change when the information is public. If you've not told your boss or your colleagues, do not post the announcement on LinkedIn. If you have told them, and you're in the transition phase of your projects, it's fair to let your network know what you're looking for and what types of introductions and referrals you seek.

Transitioning to the Next Position

According to Chris Sanchez (USN, Ret.), "You are no longer in the Department of Defense. You don't have to stay at your job/company if you don't want to. Now that you are more comfortable with being outside of the military, it's time to start improving your fighting position."

When Sanchez shared those sentiments with me, he emphasized that veterans must realize the battle is not the mission anymore. "Veterans are used to fighting for a purpose bigger than themselves," he said, "and now we need them to look after themselves."

As you leave your first employer, business venture, or school, you'll want to put yourself and your family first as you consider what you'll do next. What's best for you, and how can you make that happen?

Your next employer may repeat the onboarding process, ensuring you can leave the culture and processes of your past employer behind and learn new systems and culture. This employer may ask you to share insights and information from your last job to give them competitive edge in their own business. The employer may also ask that you start at the beginning, just like everyone else.

Your second move after leaving the military may feel very much like your first one. Although you have some civilian work experience now and have been detached from the military for a period of time, you may have many of the same feelings as you had on the last day you drove away from your last duty station.

For your new job, follow the same principles and steps laid out in this book for learning your new role, building and maintaining relationships, establishing credibility, and asking for help. In fact, with each career change you'll experience, those steps are relevant and useful.

In Closing

Understand that change is inevitable and natural. It doesn't mean you've failed or missed some important information. Over the course of your career, you'll make decisions for many reasons, and if those reasons change, you might have to adjust.

Keep the focus on you and your career development. Stay committed to continual growth and improvement, looking at your skills, talents, interests, and abilities and whether you're feeling a sense of purpose and meaning in your career.

When you do need to make a change, recognize that leaving your job can bring up feelings of frustration, disappointment, disillusionment, anger, and confusion. Perhaps you chose a job for the wrong reasons. Maybe you didn't have a career path in mind, a strong personal brand, or a well-developed support system to hold you accountable and guide you. Maybe the company you signed on with misled you or ran into trouble.

Life happens. Change happens. Your civilian career will not follow the predictable structure of your career in uniform. That brings challenge but also tremendous opportunity.

You are now in a position to be in control over your future. You can change jobs if you aren't happy, thriving, or learning and seek something different. *You* frame the narrative of your life. Create a story that provides opportunity to advance based on your contributions.

You have control and options now. You don't have to stay where you're not valued, appreciated, or revered. There is a company out there looking for someone exactly like you. If you've evaluated all the options to bring your best to work and your current employer isn't meeting you there, make a change. Get comfortable with this idea. You'll experience change many times in your career.

INDEX

CPSIA information can be obtained
at www.ICGtesting.com
Printed in the USA
JSHW051738220920
8136JS00001B/1